ECHOES FROM CALVARY

MEDITATIONS ON

FRANZ JOSEPH HAYDN'S

The Seven Last Words of Christ

EDITED BY

RICHARD YOUNG

ROWMAN & LITTLEFIELD PUBLISHERS, INC.

Lanham • Boulder • New York • Toronto • Oxford

The meditations by Raymond E. Brown are used by permission of the Associated Sulpicians of the United States, Baltimore, Maryland. All rights reserved. The meditation by Billy Graham is used by permission of the Billy Graham Evangelistic Association, Charlotte, North Carolina. All rights reserved. The meditation by Martin Luther King Jr. is reprinted by arrangement with the Estate of Martin Luther King Jr., c/o Writers House as agent for the proprietor, New York, New York.

The photo on the book cover was taken by Blake Milteer and used by permission.

ROWMAN & LITTLEFIELD PUBLISHERS, INC.

Published in the United States of America
by Rowman & Littlefield Publishers, Inc.
A wholly owned subsidiary of The Rowman & Littlefield Publishing Group, Inc.
4501 Forbes Boulevard, Suite 200, Lanham, Maryland 20706
www.rowmanlittlefield.com

PO Box 317; Oxford; OX2 9RU, UK

Distributed by National Book Network

British Library Cataloguing in Publication Information Available

Library of Congress Cataloging-in-Publication Data

Echoes from Calvary : meditations on Franz Joseph Haydn's The seven last words of Christ / edited by Richard Young.
    p.   cm.
Includes bibliographical references.
ISBN 0-7425-4384-6 (pbk. : alk. paper)
    1. Haydn, Joseph, 1732–1809. Sieben letzten Worte unseres Erlösers am Kreuze.
    2. Jesus Christ—Seven last words. I. Young, Richard, 1946 Dec. 30–

ML410.H4E3 2004
232.96'35—dc22   2004016889

Printed in the United States of America

∞™ The paper used in this publication meets the minimum requirements of American National Standard for Information Sciences—Permanence of Paper for Printed Library Materials, ANSI/NISO Z39.48-1992.

As God has given me a cheerful heart,
may He forgive me for serving Him cheerfully.
—FRANZ JOSEPH HAYDN

CONTENTS

"I THIRST."

"IT IS FINISHED!"

"Father, into your hands I commend my spirit."

The Earthquake

A MUSICAL
AND SPIRITUAL
ODYSSEY

RICHARD YOUNG

ANSWERS AND QUESTIONS

A chemistry textbook is an unlikely place to read about the death of the writer Gertrude Stein. Even more improbable is that it could provide insight into Franz Joseph Haydn's Good Friday masterpiece, *The Seven Last Words of Christ*. But since science and music have much in common, an account that contributes to our understanding of one may shed light on the other, and in so doing may even help address larger questions. Therefore the chapter entitled "The Study of Matter" in *Chemistry* by Nobel Prize winner Michell Sienko and Robert Plane is not such an inappropriate starting point for this inquiry. According to the story, loved ones were gathered around Stein's bed paying their final respects when suddenly she blurted out, "What's the answer?" Perplexed and slightly embarrassed, the well-wishers exchanged silent, knowing looks. But after gazing intently, challengingly, into every pair of eyes, she asked more gently, "Well then, what is the question?" And then she died.

For many of us, life's most important answers are elusive. They can also seem a bit diluted unless we "earn" them through our own discovery process. If we simply accept someone else's conclusions, dutifully commit them to memory, then cleverly access them at appropriate moments, it feels like we are wearing someone else's shoes. They may be the right size, they may even look good, but they feel uncomfortable because they have not been shaped by our own steps and missteps. Knowledge can often accrue through conscientious, faithful memorization. But insight almost always requires a more personal investment. The path is usually indirect and littered with incorrect hypotheses and false positives, and always the daunting specter of self-doubt lurks in the shadows. But even before the destination is reached, we appreciate that the process itself can yield a certain assurance. As we discern which questions to ask, as we learn how to ask them more intelligently and creatively, we see that the answers become not only more obvious but more valuable.

There are many types of inquiries, each of which beckons in its own special way. While science relies on its "scientific method," religion and philosophy invite "spiritual journeys." Each can be frustrated by the other's dependence, or lack of dependence, on empirical data. Meanwhile, music's "creative process," which enables composers to give animation to their inspiration, borrows from both. Its calculations can be mind-boggling, as in Arnold Schoenberg's use of the twelve-tone system in his fourth string quartet, or Béla Bartók's application of the Fibonacci series in *Music for Strings, Percussion, and Celesta.* But at the same time it can transcend its technical complexities by inexplicably reducing us to tears—tears whose saltiness need not be lab-tested to be "tasted." We are thus reminded that not all thought must be analyzed to be meaningful. And not all inquiries must be scientific to be enlightening. Because music can relate to both the scientific and the spiritual worlds, and can bridge the gap between them, it can be particularly useful to all concerned. It is more than an expression of the inner self, far more than a beautiful and engaging background accompaniment to life's experiences. As an art, a craft, a science, and a metaphor, music can also provide the basis for challenging theological, philosophical, metaphysical, and ethical discourse. While many composers have sought to reconcile its diverse and sometimes contradictory elements, few have succeeded as convincingly as Haydn did in *The Seven Last Words of Christ.*

QUESTIONS OF BALANCE

Since composers must make so many conscious decisions during every phase of their work, their creative process is necessarily intellectual, practical, pragmatic, and rational—qualities that later lend themselves to analysis. Nevertheless it can be effectively argued that the most compelling attributes of great music have little to do with those things that can be lucidly accounted for and discussed. More important, music has a "spiritual" core which defies analysis and which can sometimes be that much more persuasive as a result. The creative process thus seeks to achieve a balance between the intellectual and the emotional, the practical and the impractical, the pragmatic and the impulsive, and even the rational and the irrational. Though composers may not always find an *equal* balance, it is not coincidental that the music that is most nourishing is usually that which comes closest to achieving such a balance—music that challenges and ultimately satisfies both the mind and the heart. But because it is so much easier to talk logically about logical things, and since it can be awkward to speak emotionally about emotional things, the analysis of music tends to focus on only one side of the balance. How then can we fully appreciate the creative process if we only effectively address part of it? The answer is to embrace the notion that the heart has a "logic" all its own. Though it speaks a "language" that the mind may find inexact, it can articulate things that the mind cannot fully grasp, and that the mind's language can only begin to express.

The debate on the roles of the mind and the heart, of science and religion, has been raging for centuries. Galileo's conviction that the universe can be explained solely by mathematics naturally put him on a collision course with the Catholic Church. With his invention of the telescope in 1609—nearly half a century *after* my beautiful Peregrino di Zanetto viola was made!—the Copernican hypothesis was proven, thus answering certain questions but creating a host of others. How does one account for "truth," "meaning," or "integrity"—metaphysical issues with ethical ramifications that are beyond the scope of mathematics? Wade

Rowland asks if we are not sacrificing more than we gain when we apply the scientific method to all circumstances.

> Are we happier in our day-to-day lives than our ancestors, or merely more comfortable? Are the lives we lead more worthy of respect, or less? Is our world, taken all in all, a better place than theirs? To what extent are the advances made over the past four hundred years in social and economic justice attributable to science? In what degree have they been made in spite of science, which teaches the social efficacy of natural selection and survival of the fittest?[1]

A similar debate resonates in the music world. Paul Hindemith, one of the most intelligent and versatile musicians of the twentieth century, expressed his misgivings on analysis in no uncertain terms.

> I cannot provide analyses of my compositions because I do not know how to explain music in just a few words. I'd rather write a new piece in the time it takes. Besides, I believe that for people with ears my stuff is easy to grasp, and so an analysis is superfluous. But for people without ears, overpasses for jackasses are useless.[2]

The nonverbal arts often take over at the very moment inadequate words begin to stutter. Because words are the currency of literature and poetry, it is not surprising that even their most compelling examples have difficulty conveying the full impact of art's spiritual essence. But there *are* occasional instances where words come close to conveying art's indefinable spirituality, such as this extraordinary passage by W. Somerset Maugham, which describes the impression made upon him by a painting.

> It [conveyed] an awful sense of the infinity of space and of the endlessness of time . . . [of] something strangely alive . . . as though [it was] created in a stage of the earth's dark history when things were not irrevocably fixed to their forms. . . . It gave me the impression you get when you are sitting next door to a room that you know is empty, but in which, you know not why, you have a dreadful consciousness

that notwithstanding there is someone. You scold yourself; you know it is only your nerves—and yet, and yet . . .[3]

Some empirical minds are unsatisfied by this kind of language. Despite its emotional appeal, they consider it vague and imprecise. But after chewing on some of the lines from *Alterwise by Owl-light* by Dylan Thomas—e.g. "Abaddon in the hangnail cracked from Adam / And, from his fork, a dog among the fairies / The atlas-eater with a jaw for news, / Bit out the mandrake with to-morrow's scream."[4]—who could possibly say that *this* language lacks specificity and precision? For here is an altogether different standard of precision that is no less accurate than many scientific measurements. But whereas scientists' calculations are trusted for their impersonal objectivity, poets' meticulous probings of the inner self are valued for their intensely personal subjectivity. Because these standards measure different things in different ways, they are both valuable. Each contributes to a balance that is unattainable without the other. This helps explain why a Bach fugue sounds even more compelling when one understands its complicated mechanisms, and why these mechanisms are even more satisfying when one finally basks in the indescribable beauty of their manifestation. A similar balance of precision and imagination, of premeditation and unleashed abandon, is found on a miniature scale in the *Five Pieces, Op. 5* by Anton Webern, and on a grander scale in both the late string quartets of Beethoven, and the quartets of Elliott Carter. One might say that the "languages" of Thomas, Bach, Webern, Beethoven, and Carter—not unlike the "language" of faith— are *passionately precise* because of this special balance.

These illustrations are provided as a caution to fellow wayfarers to neither overvalue nor undervalue certain road signs along the way simply because they do (or don't) lend themselves to the mind's unique form of analysis. Though the mind has an exactitude that the heart may ignore, that does not mean one should listen less carefully to the heart's specific urgings. Since the mind and the heart have altogether different vocabularies to express their very different priorities, one must take care to speak the appropriate languages when asking the questions. While this can be a useful reminder to those with faith questions, it can also be especially valuable to anyone examining *The Seven Last Words of*

Christ—a work that cries out with passionate precision, a highly personal outpouring that is a many-layered expression of Haydn's own religious faith.

The First Uncertain Steps

My relationship these many years with *The Seven Last Words of Christ* has provided the context for my ongoing spiritual odyssey. I am not a theologian, nor did I ever take a religion course in college. I am a professional musician—and a person who struggles, like most others, to find meaningful answers to questions that often seem unanswerable. When this pilgrimage began I was like the person described by Harvard professor Peter Gomes: "I always know where I am. It is where I am going that is the problem." My prospects for progress were enhanced, however, by the knowledgeable and insightful group of theologians and pastors I have been honored to meet along the way. With the Gospels of Matthew, Mark, Luke, and John providing the context, and with Haydn's music setting the tone, these often extraordinary men and women have helped me formulate and clarify the relevant questions. We expect insight from world-class scholars like Raymond Brown, Martin Marty, and David Tracy, or from dynamic preachers like Billy Graham, Jeremiah Wright, and Martin Luther King Jr. But we also happen upon inspiration in less likely places in the meditations within these pages related by relatively unknown individuals such as Kelly Clem, Seiichi Michael Yasutake, and Yvonne Hawkins. Each has a story to tell, a story that may be related with the dazzling rhetorical flair of an Andrew Greeley or a Peter Gomes, with the poetic gift of a Dorothy McRae-McMahon, a William Spofford, or an Elizabeth-Anne Stewart, or with the unvarnished eloquence of a Willie Cusic or a Rita Simó. By the end of this collection each has contributed to a rich, multitextured mosaic whose individual pieces somehow fit together and complement one another in a manner that enables onlookers to proceed with greater confidence, sensing that the journey's important questions and answers are within reach.

Franz Joseph Haydn is considered "the father of the string quartet," and of his more than eighty opuses for this genre *The Seven Last Words of Christ* is probably his greatest. But for reasons that will soon become clear, it is seldom performed by today's touring ensembles. Nevertheless my group, the Vermeer String Quartet, decided to program the "secular concert version" throughout the 1987–1988 season. That is, we offered only the music, without the spoken meditations based on Jesus' final utterances that were originally specified by Haydn. The piece occupied the second half of one of our tour programs; the first half consisted of the *Variations and Scherzo* by Felix Mendelssohn and the second string quartet by Benjamin Britten. Despite its incredible beauty, we found that the Haydn made a wearying impression in this setting. In part, this is because eight of its nine movements are slow, and though each has its own distinctive character, the total effect can be numbing. Moreover, with no recovery time between each of these very intense movements, we found that it was physically and emotionally exhausting to perform. Players and listeners alike felt overwhelmed. As we trudged offstage to the polite applause of the worn-out audience following one such occasion, our cellist muttered in frustration, "These people just had the experience of their lives and don't even know it!"

Later that season we were hired to perform *The Seven Last Words of Christ* in England with the Shakespearian actor, Sir Alec McGowan, as "narrator." This marked the first time we performed the work with spoken introductions. However, McGowan took what the concert organizers calculated was a safe, "nonreligious" approach. Between the movements, instead of quoting Jesus, he read selections from essays by John Donne. But by trying so hard not to offend, the whole point of the piece was missed. Tina Turner's question, rhetorically posed, echoed in my ears as we packed up our instruments afterwards: "What's love got to do with it?" Clearly we had to find another way.

The most obvious solution was to observe Haydn's own instructions, which meant putting back the references to the particular scripture texts that inspired this music. But most classical musicians these days are reluctant to be identified with anything that is "too religious." Exceptions are made with certain works, such as Handel's *Messiah*, which appears to have transcended its original concept to such an extent that religious and nonreligious people alike seem immune to the meaning of the words they are singing. With voices raised with commitment and passion, with tears often streaming down their cheeks, they belt out the famous *Hallelujah Chorus,* often without regard for what and whom they are actually praising! With *The Seven Last Words of Christ*, however, the possibility for ambiguity is nonexistent when it is presented as Haydn enjoined. Though our minds may wander in "spiritual" but not necessarily "religious" directions as the music washes over us, time and again we are brought back to the reality of this work by spoken meditations whose purpose is to focus attention on the particular words, religious words, that served as this music's inspiration.

Professional musicians need not apologize for the motivation of this work any more than they should make excuses for the motivation of any other work they perform. Often we speak of our responsibility to learn everything possible about whatever it was that compelled composers to write their masterpieces. We discuss the various ways our interpretations are colored by this knowledge, whether the composer is Mozart, Beethoven, Smetana, Alban Berg or Leoš Janáček. Even when we do not share a composer's particular motivation, it is our duty to find appropriate means for it to influence our realization of the music. With *all* music, we should make every effort to understand and respect the genesis of its inspiration—its underlying motivation. With *The Seven Last Words of Christ,* there is simply no question what inspired Haydn, or what our responsibility should be.

So much for the performers. Do listeners have to be Christians in order to be substantially nourished by this music? The answer is a resounding no, for this extraordinary opus is able to transcend its roots and resonate far beyond Christian sanctuaries. Jane Addams, the woman who founded Chicago's Hull-House, wrote about "the common human nature" of people. She observed that "the things that make men [and women] alike are stronger and more primitive than the things that separate them."[5] It is this "common human nature" that enables Haydn's masterpiece to provide spiritual sustenance for all sorts of people, regardless of their backgrounds—not only for Christians, not only for religious non-Christians, but even for those who would call themselves nonreligious. That Haydn was able to satisfy the "thirst" of the faithful, yet provide so many ways to inspire, challenge, and nourish others, is remarkable.

REVELATIONS AND RE-REVELATIONS

On April 1, 1988, the Vermeer String Quartet did a special "live" Good Friday broadcast of *The Seven Last Words of Christ* that permanently changed our relationship with this piece. It was arranged by Norman Pellegrini, the visionary program director of WFMT radio in Chicago, who insisted on following Haydn's original format. This meant finding one or more speakers to present the meditations that would be heard before each section of music. The more obvious choices included the Catholic archbishop of Chicago, high-profile pastors of local churches, or religion professors from Loyola University, DePaul University, and The University of Chicago Divinity School. But I chose to go in a different direction. Just as Haydn reached out beyond traditional boundaries, it seemed right to look beyond the obvious mainstream choices. I decided to invite a pastor from one of the community's less advantaged neighborhoods, someone who is a colorful and charismatic preacher and whose style is joined with substance. I wanted someone whose followers were not necessarily classical music enthusiasts, but who would listen with open hearts and minds if for no other reason than that their beloved pastor was involved.

For far too long, classical music in general and chamber music in particular have been perceived as elitist music—and for very good reason. Since Haydn's early days when he was a composer for the court of Prince Esterházy, this kind of music has been intended for those who can well afford "the finer things" in life. The profile of a chamber music concertgoer today is still a privileged white person over fifty-five years old. The parking lots at most of our concerts are filled with new Lexus and Mercedes automobiles, not Chevy Cavaliers and Nissan Sentras. As I look out at the audience from my seat onstage in virtually any city in the world where the Vermeer performs, I see a sea of white faces. Minorities, even affluent minorities, are rarely present. There are many reasons for this, not the least of which is that chamber music events are often so unimaginatively promoted, and classical music education in recent decades has been so woefully inadequate. Nevertheless I have always felt that the very best examples of chamber music, even those that were written over two centuries ago and intended for the very rich, have an inherent appeal that can transcend today's sociological differences. Thanks to Norman Pellegrini and WFMT, here was an opportunity to put this belief to the test.

A friend who provided psychological counseling for inner city Chicago children suggested Pastor T. L. Barrett. His church, the Life Center Church of God in Christ, is located less than a mile west of The University of Chicago. Its immediate surroundings, however, are worlds apart from the university's "golden rectangle" in terms of style and affluence. Almost all American cities have areas like this, formerly thriving neighborhoods that now house more despair than promise. Their "multicultural vitality" is an inspiring concept to some passers-by, but for others this translates to "lock your car doors." Pastor Barrett's church stands on the corner of 55th Street and Indiana Avenue—the very corner where he stood more than thirty years ago and pledged to turn his life around, having been kicked out of school for the last time. His father had died when he was sixteen and he had grown up in the depressing, demeaning, and dangerous Chicago Housing Authority "projects." And yet he has become one of the community's most influential leaders— and a remarkably gifted preacher.

A couple of weeks before the broadcast we met in a fancy restaurant in Chicago's Loop to talk through his meditations over dinner. It was the kind of quiet, intimate setting that encourages muted conversation. Barrett was dressed in black except for his white clerical collar, and though he was not the only African American in the restaurant, he was the only black patron. Later he told me he had trouble flagging down a taxi to take him back to the South Side. After dinner, over coffee, he suggested that he read out loud the final version of his texts, and suddenly before my eyes he was transformed into Preacher Barrett. Though his readings were not particularly loud, his passion commanded the attention of every single person in the restaurant. When he had finished I looked around to see all eyes upon us: patrons, waiters, waitresses, the maitre-d', even the coat-check girl. No doubt about it, I had found my preacher.

The broadcast was electric. Somehow we transformed each other. For the four of us in the Vermeer, it was a re-revelation. Though we knew the music so very well, we had never before been obliged to relate to it in its intended context. It was also a new experience for Rev.

Barrett, since his previous exposure to Haydn had been practically nonexistent. I was later told that as he listened to the music from his separate studio, tears formed in his eyes. It was estimated that there were more than ten thousand first-time listeners to WFMT that evening. Most were enthralled—but not all. Norman Pellegrini read me a letter from "a loyal listener" who complained about "the appropriateness of the speaker." Yes, we had touched a nerve—all sorts of them.

In the years that followed, we presented *The Seven Last Words of Christ* during Holy Week in various churches throughout Chicago, each time with a different speaker. In early 1994 I suggested to my three Vermeer colleagues that we record the piece. But instead of having just one speaker do all seven meditations, I wanted to consider having a different person for each "word," thus enabling us to present a variety of perspectives. Mathias Tacke, our second violinist, whose father had been a minister in his native Germany, expressed concern about the lack of continuity that might result from a group of such different individuals. We weighed the pros and cons, and finally went forward with the plan that, coincidentally, has now made possible this collection of meditations.

The next step was to select the speakers. I wanted the group to include not only world-renowned religious figures, but a few whose presence would underscore the belief that the message's messengers need not be famous to be convincing. The group consisted of Father Raymond Brown, Dr. Martin Marty, Rev. Kelly Clem, Evangelist Billy Graham, Elder Dallin Oaks, Father Virgil Elizondo, Pastor T. L. Barrett, and Rev. Martin Luther King Jr., with Jason Robards reading the *Introduction*. Rev. Theodore Hesburgh, President Emeritus of the University of Notre Dame, later wrote, "It is difficult to imagine a more appropriate group of theologians and preachers for the Vermeer's recording of *The Seven Last Words of Christ*. The makeup of this group suggests not only a certain moral authority, but also a spirit of inclusiveness—just as the biblical message itself is meant to exclude no one. At the same time, in a most personal and effective manner, it reflects our religious and social diversity."

It was clear from the outset that this project would be (in the words of our cellist, Marc Johnson) "Richard's baby." Though my three colleagues welcomed the idea of making the recording, they were not particularly interested in taking on the accompanying tasks. For each of our other recordings, we have been hired by an established company such as Teldec, Orfeo, Cedille, and Naxos. The roles are clear and nonoverlapping. We play the music and have limited input regarding editing decisions, and the recording company takes care of everything else. But that could not happen this time. In order to ensure the participation of certain speakers, I had to promise that none of the decisions regarding the final version of the recording would be left to anyone with a commercial interest. So I formed a not-for-profit corporation, Alden Productions Inc. (named for my late father), under whose auspices every aspect of the project has been undertaken. Essentially I have been doing this by myself, from the company's "corporate headquarters"—my little upstairs office at home, across the hall from my practice room.

I hired Larry Rock, now the audio engineer for the New York Philharmonic, to do the recording, editing, and mastering. Larry also assumed the role of "session director" since we lacked an in-studio "producer." He recommended Bob Atkins of Advanced Audio Technology to coordinate the manufacturing and packaging of the CDs and cassettes. The recording sessions took place in May 1994 on the stage of the concert hall at Northern Illinois University where the Vermeer is the quartet-in-residence. This location was chosen for two reasons. First, I wanted a sonority that was "church-like" rather than a "studio" sound. Second, it wouldn't cost us anything.

The spoken meditations by Billy Graham and Martin Luther King Jr. were excerpted from previously recorded sermons that are now housed in archives. Finding and obtaining permission for these historic tapes required a good bit of sleuthing, persistence, and patience. But in the end it was well worth it, and I remain grateful to the various people associated with the organizations that continue to promote the work of these two great men. The other meditations were recorded in the spring and summer of 1994. For logistical reasons they were done in different studios across the country. Kelly Clem did hers in Alabama, Raymond Brown in California, Virgil Elizondo in Texas, Dallin Oaks in Utah, and T. L. Barrett and Martin Marty in Illinois. Jason Robards recorded the *Introduction* in Connecticut.

It is important to carefully choose the visual image that will appear on the front of any CD jewel box. But I had no idea until much later just how revealing—literally revealing—the cover of our recording of *The Seven Last Words of Christ* would eventually prove to be. Of the thousands of works of art that depict the crucifixion of Jesus, I was most tempted to use Salvador Dali's *Crucifixion,* a sanitized and bloodless depiction which actually compounds the horror. As much as I adore this picture, I hesitated, since I did not want to suggest in any way that this CD is "for Christians only," an attitude that certain iconic depictions of the Cross can encourage. But while I wanted an image that would convey the shock and terror of crucifixion, I also wanted it to enable Christians to imagine the greater significance of the Cross. In other words, I wanted a crucifixion that also suggested the Crucifixion.

Finding nothing that satisfied these requirements, I decided to "compose" a photograph that would view the Cross not from such a distance that its message-sending shape would be apparent, but up close—painfully close. It would show one of the beams of a wooden cross that (one could imagine) had previously been used in a crucifixion, now splintering and rotting, but in whose cracks and crevices there are green specks of new life. And to drive home the point, there would be a nail—a cruel, rusty iron nail to which flesh is no longer clinging. I hired a talented young photographer, Blake Milteer, to take the picture that is featured on the front cover of this volume of meditations. But no ordinary nail or beam would do. Blake's girlfriend, Sarah, came up with the nail, I know not where. And after a painstaking search I found the ideal piece of rotting wood, hidden under mounds of unmentionable garbage in the town dump in Camden, Maine, where the Vermeer plays summer concerts.

Months later, as I casually glanced at the stunning photograph on the front cover of our CD, something suddenly caught my attention—something I had never noticed before. Just to the right of the iron nail at a slight diagonal angle was a distinct pattern formed by splinters in the wood. A cross! And just above the place where the two beams intersect at right angles there appeared a face, a face with a striking resemblance to Jesus! Now as suddenly as it had appeared, the image disappeared into the wooden splinters. But as my vision refocused, there it was again—no doubt about it—and every time since when I have looked at this photo, that face stares out at me.

13

The following summer when I returned to Maine for more concerts, I went back to the place in the woods where I had left that piece of wood after the photo session. I had to know: was the face really there? Or had it been a once-in-a-lifetime illusion created by the camera angle, the lighting, or a dozen other manifestations of chance? I finally found the beam, almost completely hidden by undergrowth and vines, even more decayed and bug-infested than before. I located the exact place where the face had been visible in the photograph, but it was nowhere to be seen. Not exactly a Shroud of Turin, it nevertheless has provided a certain aura of mystery to the journey. In this instance, at least, I am comfortable with Herman Melville's explanation in the allegory of "The Mat-maker," which describes "chance, free will, and necessity—no wise incompatible—all interweavingly working together."[6] It was as if Blake Milteer had become my "impulsive, indifferent"[7] Queequeg when he unknowingly snapped the shutter at precisely the moment that enabled the face to be revealed. And who could argue that all the while it was indeed "God's foot upon the treadle of the loom"?[8]

Shortly after our recording of *The Seven Last Words of Christ* was released, it received a Grammy nomination in the Classical Field as the Best Chamber Music Performance of 1995. Not bad for a tiny independent label that had only one "title" in its catalogue. The final competition for the Grammy against the industry's corporate giants had all the earmarks of David versus Goliath. Unfortunately this time the giant (Sony) prevailed. Nevertheless, the Grammy exposure fueled a great deal of interest. Through broadcasts to an estimated sixty million listeners worldwide during Holy Week that year, it demonstrated a unique appeal that reached far beyond the traditional classical music audience. It is fair to say that our CD both revealed and re-revealed Haydn's opus to a surprising number of people.

RECORDING PARTNERS

There are many wonderful stories I could tell about the speakers on our CD of *The Seven Last Words of Christ.* Here are three of the more memorable ones.

One of the two liberties I took with Haydn's original format was to include a spoken introduction just prior to the *Introduction* movement.

(The other was to include, just before the final *Earthquake* movement, the relevant scripture verses from Matthew that describe the earthquake that immediately followed Jesus' death.) I wanted the spoken introduction to tell the Good Friday story in a way that faithfully described the events recorded in the Gospels that led up to Jesus' Seven Last Words. Since this portion didn't have to reflect a particular religious viewpoint, what I needed was someone to assume the role of storyteller rather than commentator. I could think of no one more appropriate than one of the great actors of our time, Jason Robards. If the key to real estate is "location," the key to hiring a famous actor is "access." And it just so happened that I knew someone, Jim Helfrich, whose son had married into Robards' family. Many patient letters and nervous phone calls later, he agreed. And like every one of the other speakers, he generously consented to do the recording for free.

Since Jason Robards lived in Southport, Connecticut, he preferred to record his introduction in a nearby Westport studio. Because I had a concert in Chicago the day of his recording, I could not be there with him, as I would have liked. Instead we communicated throughout the session via an open telephone line. I had faxed him the "script" in advance, and as the engineer set microphone levels, I could hear him practicing his lines. It was fascinating—so similar to the way musicians practice passages over and over. First one way, then another. Louder, then softer. Slower, then faster. Always with varying degrees of calculated intensity. When he was finally ready to "perform," all previous "calculations" were set aside so his instincts could take over. And how Robards took over! For me, the feeling was not unlike hearing another violinist or violist perform one of my own compositions. Though the inflection might not have been exactly the way I would have done it, it was compelling nonetheless, perhaps even more so since there was now a hint of danger—the result of my hearing it differently from the way I was expecting. It was a virtuoso performance every bit as great as Robards' Academy Award-winning performances in *Julia* and *All the President's Men,* or his memorable roles in *Long Day's Journey into Night* and *A Moon for the Misbegotten.* After the recording session we visited a bit, and I asked him if his own religious convictions had influenced his decision to do this. He chuckled and said, "My wife is Catholic."

It was Rev. Kelly Clem who first helped me see the "human" face of *The Seven Last Words of Christ.* Of all those who contributed meditations for the CD, she was the least well known. But for fate, she would have been unfamiliar to just about everyone. A huge tornado changed all that the moment it tore into her church in rural Alabama during the 1994 Palm Sunday service. Portions of the wall and roof collapsed on the congregation, injuring many and killing twenty people, including Pastor Clem's own four-year-old daughter, Hannah. When I saw Kelly on the evening news a day or two later, standing amid the rubble of her church, her faith undaunted by the tragedy, I knew I had to find her. Who better to express what it must have been like for Mary, who stood helplessly at the foot of the Cross and watched *her* child die?

After many phone calls I reached her and explained what I had in mind. Initially flattered by the invitation, she hesitated, since she felt unworthy in the company of such renowned theologians as Raymond Brown and Martin Marty, to say nothing of the legendary Billy Graham and Martin Luther King Jr. But I reminded her of the uniqueness of her perspective as both a pastor and a mother—one who had paid a dear price for her special insight. Shortly thereafter, in August 1994, I traveled to Jacksonville State University to meet her and to record her meditation.

The university radio station's recording studio was spartan. Though the air conditioning was cranked up all the way on this scorching summer day, the air was uncomfortably hot and stale. There was also an audible noise from the barely adequate fluorescent light. Since I suspected the session could be difficult, I wanted to sit next to Kelly to coax her through her meditation. But this was not so easily done, since the single microphone was permanently mounted in a console designed to accommodate only one person. When we wedged our plastic folding chairs into that very narrow space, we were uncomfortably pressed together. But if either of us felt awkward at first, this was quickly forgotten as we became wrapped up in the inspiration of the moment.

Kelly had written down a couple of short paragraphs in advance. I still have that piece of paper on which the carefully spaced words were neatly printed in ink. The first few readings were stiff and self-conscious—not unlike the first "takes" of a Vermeer recording session. This all changed after the engineer reported that he was picking up the hum from the fluorescent light. We had no choice but to turn it off, leaving only the faint glow from the control room on the other side of the glass—barely enough light for us to see each other, but not enough for Kelly to make out the words she had written on the paper. I reminded her that she didn't need her notes, that if she stumbled we could go back and do it again. She should just close her eyes and do it from memory, allowing the heart to set the tone and pace. What emerged from this brave young woman was pure, unadulterated love. With her husband, Dale, occasionally adding encouragement from his seat in the shadows a few feet away, the closest she came to breaking down was when she looked over and saw my quiet tears. She gently scolded, "Now you pull yourself together, Richard"—as if to say, *"If I can get through this, so can you. Behold your sister!"* To this day, Kelly Clem's meditation is the one that touches the most hearts, the one that evokes the most personal comments from those who describe how the recording has so deeply affected them. That is because Kelly conveys the kind of quiet urgency that can only come from having lived these words. But at what price!

Some individuals are so famous that all they need is one name: Cher, Madonna, Tiger, and Hillary. Even the classical music world has one: Midori. The religion community certainly has one: Marty, more formally known as Dr. Martin E. Marty. When I was putting together the CD, everyone who advised me insisted that any list that purports to include some of the most prominent religious figures of our time *must* include Dr. Marty. It wasn't hard to track him down. He is listed in the local phone book. I was prepared to have to explain not only who I was, but what Haydn's *The Seven Last Words of Christ* is all about. After only one ring, the sharp, crisp voice answered: "Marty." The quick conversation went something like this.

> *Richard*: "Good afternoon, Dr. Marty. This is Richard Young, and I'm the violist of the Vermeer String Quartet. We're . . ."
> *Marty*: "Yes, I know you. Or at least I know your playing. Wonderful. I probably have some of your CDs right here. What's up?"

Richard (flattered): "We are recording *The Seven Last Words of Christ,* and I'm calling to ask if you'd be interested in doing one of the spoken meditations."

Marty: "Be happy to. Thanks for asking. By the way, which version are you doing, the one by Haydn or the one by Heinrich Schutz?"

There I was, speaking with one of the most celebrated theologians in the English-speaking world—already a daunting experience. But since the topic was *music,* I was reasonably confident. After all, this was my specialty, not his. My primary concern was to explain things clearly enough so that a nonmusician could immediately understand. But all of a sudden I felt utterly disoriented and inadequate, for I had only now learned *from him* that there exists a version of *The Seven Last Words of Christ* by Heinrich Schutz! Within my first half minute with Dr. Marty, I had thus learned what *everyone* learns sooner than later: that one should never assume there are any limits whatsoever to his expertise. Incidentally, I am now familiar with the Schutz version. Dr. Marty loaned me his recording.

I won't recite here Martin Marty's long list of credits. Instead, let me mention what, for me, is one of his greatest and most unique gifts. He is able to discuss complicated ideas in a refreshingly uncomplicated manner that enables even nonexperts to understand perfectly. Yet he never dilutes the substance or compromises the essence of these often-difficult concepts. Like Mozart, he can convey the most profound thoughts and sentiments with disarming simplicity without ever sounding simplistic. There is no hint of "dumbing down" in his explanations. They are so crisp, concise, and clear that after one hears or reads them, one wonders why things were previously so murky. And because of his easygoing kindness and humility, one can be constantly challenged and even humbled without ever feeling diminished or demeaned. Of all the generous souls I have met on this journey, no one has taught me more than Marty.

MAKING EVERY WORD COUNT

In 1997 we found a permanent home for our annual Chicago presentations: Rockefeller Memorial Chapel, on the campus of The University of Chicago. This beautiful historic landmark has a dignity that is probably not unlike the church in Cadiz, Spain, where *The Seven Last Words of Christ* was first performed. The ceilings of this 1,400-seat structure are high, the lighting is simple, and the acoustics are lively but surprisingly well integrated. Just as important is the allure of Rockefeller's rich interfaith tradition, which has helped us to attract an unusually diverse audience to these performances. Indeed, it is different from any audience for whom my string quartet performs, anywhere in the world. It reflects virtually every segment of the community—young and old, advantaged and disadvantaged, religious and nonreligious. Joining regular concertgoers are many people who do not often attend classical music events, including some who may be hearing a string quartet perform for the very first time. Numerous families attend, as well as groups from schools, universities, senior homes, community organizations, and churches. The fact that all these people are there together, each inspired in his or her own way and listening with such obvious involvement, makes the experience that much more meaningful. Haydn himself would undoubtedly have been pleased, given his expressed wish that *every* listener, regardless of his or her personal circumstances, "will be moved to the very depths of his soul."

Over the years I have invited dozens of speakers, including some of the Chicago area's most important scholars, pastors, and community leaders. Through their different religious perspectives, their various ethnic backgrounds, their diverse preaching and lecturing styles, even their unique voices and accents, they reflect our American landscape. One thing they have in common, however, is their difficulty dealing with the two-minute time limit that we require for each meditation. "It's not preachin' the way it's supposed to be," one veteran pastor grumbled. It imposes restraints to which academics and preachers alike are unaccustomed. Where else must they take care to avoid digressions, asides, anecdotes, footnotes, and embellishments? Certainly not when standing before a class of college doctoral students or a packed congregation of worshippers! No wonder many of our guest speakers express initial discomfort with the time restriction. Still, almost all manage to find ways to say what needs to be said by making every word count.

A memorable afternoon spent at the Benjamin Britten Library in Aldeburgh, England, comes to mind. Aldeburgh is a quaint British town northeast of London, on the North Sea coast. It hosts an important summer music festival which the great composer, Benjamin Britten, established a half century ago. I asked the library's curator if I could examine the manuscript of Britten's third string quartet, his final work, composed in 1975 on his deathbed. This is a piece I know well and have performed many times with the Vermeer. Nevertheless, I was unprepared for the powerful impression these pages made on me. Bedridden and very weak, Britten was in constant pain during those final days. Yet he insisted on completing this final opus. He sat propped up with a wooden board in his lap that served as a hard writing surface for his manuscript paper. He did not use the store-bought kind, with the five lines of the staff already printed on the page. Rather, he insisted on drawing his own lines, though even the slightest movement was now difficult.

As I studied the yellowing pages I could see evidence of the man's suffering. As the staff lines approach the right hand margin they become fainter and less steady. There is also a distinct contrast between the more boldly drawn notes near the top left side of each page and those near the bottom right margin. Because of his severe discomfort, this composer known for colorful orchestrations and florid textures was forced to economize. This helps to explain this quartet's compact proportions, the efficient touches, perhaps even the decision to write a four-voice composition rather than a symphony or an opera. There is no fat—only muscle, sinew, and bone—just the essentials. And yet this is one of Britten's most profoundly moving works, due primarily to the intimacy and vulnerability that imbue every note. While it is true that the final compositions of many composers are characterized by a return to a simpler, more fundamental, and less decorative approach—the last quartets by Beethoven, Shostakovich, and Bartók are good examples—this does not entirely explain Britten's motivation. Life's questions and answers probably *were* becoming clearer as he approached death's door, but it is also true that it was physically painful for him to embellish his music with nonessential trappings. He had no choice but to make every gesture count.

For the Vermeer's very first performance at Rockefeller Chapel in 1997, my plan was to include a contingent of three scholars from the University of Chicago. This was intended not merely as a courtesy, since this was their turf, but because it would set an exceptionally high standard for the spoken meditations. That group consisted of Martin Marty, Alison Boden, and Jean Bethke Elshtain. From time to time the university's representation has been expanded to include the brilliance of David Tracy and Andrew Greeley, plus the viewpoints of prominent individuals with previous ties to the Divinity School, such as John Buchanan and B. Herbert Martin. But that original threesome has remained the same year after year.

By this time, I had decided that our "live" performances should follow the same format as our recording—that instead of using one speaker, the meditations should be divided among various individuals. However questions have occasionally been raised about the appropriateness of this approach, as happened when we made the recording. One prominent religious figure even claimed that splitting up the words among different speakers "deprives the *treore* of any integrity." There are indeed certain risks to the many-voiced approach, including the fact that it is nearly impossible to achieve the same unity that is possible with a single speaker. Moreover "the message" may be blurred by a lack of consistency and continuity. There is a practical concern as well that some of the meditations may not measure up to the very high standard of others.

However there are certain risks associated with a single-voice approach too. For instance, one is far less likely to convey a spirit of inclusiveness, or to reflect the community's (and the ministry's) religious and social diversity, as previously suggested by Theodore Hesburgh. Is not the price of consistency and continuity too dear if the unintended result is homogeneity and conformity? While multivoice presentations may lack a unified perspective and a consistent rhetorical style, they contribute to a different kind of unity—one that also works well for democracies, despite many of the same incongruities and inconveniences: *e pluribus unum.*

Another compelling argument in favor of the approach that uses multiple speakers is the fact that the Gospel was originally communicated not by one "voice" but by four, each of which had its own unique shading, rhythm, texture, flavor, and perspective. Since having various speakers is a more accurate reflection of what is actually found in the Gospel, would one be wrong to suggest that this approach has *more* "integrity" rather than less?

In the years since the release of the recording we have performed *The Seven Last Words of Christ* dozens of times in this format, not only at Rockefeller Chapel but also throughout the United States. We have even toured the major cities in Australia, with prominent members of the Australian clergy providing meditations. Since the speakers always compose their own material, I never know quite what to expect, even though I provide clear guidelines beforehand. Fortunately I have never had to face anything more difficult than negotiating an occasional change of word or a slightly different turn of phrase in order to avoid crossing that delicate line that separates personal expressions of faith from proselytizing. The biggest challenge has been to "make every word count" by finding just the right tone. One way or another, the meditations should be interesting, inspiring, and thought provoking. And frankly, I have no interest in serving up "nutra-sweetened vinegar and gall" or "sour wine lite."

The meditations, not by accident, tend to fall into three general categories: (1) those that are intellectually (theologically) stimulating—for example, those by David Tracy, Demetri Kantzavelos, Peter Knobel, and Jean Bethke Elshtain; (2) those that are spiritually uplifting and prayerful—for example, the ones by Billy Graham, Evelyn Varboncoeur, Addie Wyatt, and Virgil Elizondo; and (3) those that have contemporary relevance and challenge our modern-day values—for example, those by Don Wycliff, Seiichi Michael Yasutaki, Willie Cusic, Gregory Dell, and Rita Simó.

Because, as Martin Marty points out, "smooth coins . . . can lose their ability to be felt,"[9] it has been important to not just dutifully "re-rub" Haydn's opus each year. Smoothed coins tend to give calloused fingers the impression that they now lack the same sensitivity they had when they first touched these coins. What is needed are not coins of a different denomination, but coins whose edges feel as sharp as ever, particularly to fingers that have been hardened by many previous rubbings. Making sure that each of our performances includes at least one or two meditations of the third type has enabled Haydn's timeless music to maintain its contemporary "edge."

In 1962 the American composer Earle Brown completed a set of works entitled *Available Forms,* in which the players are provided with a number of short musical excerpts—fixed bits of "available" material that are then improvised into "forms." Though the specific pitches and/or the general melodic shape are always provided, the tempo, rhythm, and mode of expression are left up to the performers. The resulting mosaic of sound is therefore different each time. Indeed, though each component is strictly predetermined, their always unique juxtaposition constantly re-creates the piece. It not only sounds different each time, it *is* different, even though the melodic material of each individual element is never altered. It is thus like a mobile, each of whose individual three-dimensional shapes is performed. But as these components rotate on their separate threads, as the mobile's arms rotate on theirs, and as the viewer changes perspective by shifting position, the view of the totality is never exactly the same. Moreover as the light changes, as new brilliance is focused on each element, and as new shadows are cast, both the details and the entirety are always seen in a "new light."

Our performances of *The Seven Last Words of Christ* have much in common with Brown's *Available Forms* and with mobiles. Haydn's music and Jesus' words are never-changing. But because the spoken meditations on these words are always different—and hence their juxtaposition and relationship to each other is always new—the listener's view of the totality is never the same. The music "sounds" different each time, not only because of the performers' normal human tendencies to vary each performance, but because it is always "heard" in a "new light."

Nil dictum dictum—nothing is said that has not already been said— is a traditional Latin expression that many of us learned when we were teenagers. Though Haydn's music and Jesus' words have already been "said" countless times, what they "say" in each one of our performances is always different. Consequently, each presentation invites new possibilities and issues new challenges to the musicians and speakers alike to make every note and every word count.

RESPECTING APPROPRIATE BOUNDARIES

The notion that "nothing is sacred anymore" in today's world is reinforced by the fact that performers of religiously motivated music do not always take a respectful approach. A good example of this occurred in

2002 when the music department of one of Chicago's universities presented *The Seven Last Words of Christ* on its artist series. But instead of having meditations based on Jesus' final utterances, an award-winning poet was hired to write and read nonreligious poems before each section of music. Keep in mind that it is not unusual for classical music compositions to be adapted to serve purposes other than those originally intended by the composers. Madison Avenue and Hollywood do it all the time, often very effectively. Few were bothered when they heard Strauss' *Blue Danube Waltz* in the movie *2001,* or Barber's *Adagio for Strings* in *Platoon.* No one is offended when they hear Gershwin's *Rhapsody in Blue* as a United Airlines 747 sweeps across their television screen, or when they see Olympic figure skaters perform triple axels to Bizet's *Carmen.* But certain pieces should be handled with uncommon sensitivity.

Imagine using Shostakovich's eighth string quartet—which was written in memory of the victims of fascism and war—for a propaganda film that glorifies Stalin, Mussolini, and Hitler. Imagine a performance of Copland's *Lincoln Portrait* that instead quotes the Imperial Wizard of the Ku Klux Klan. Imagine an oratorio about the horrors of the Holocaust that scraps its original text in favor of one that advances the theory that the Holocaust never occurred. Now imagine meditations for *The Seven Last Words of Christ* that are not just secular, but which are tone-deaf to the sensibilities of the faithful due to their nontheistic tone and content. This is exactly what happened here.

One can appreciate the motivation of concert performers and presenters who strive to reach a broader audience by making classical music more accessible. One can relate to the idealistic motivation of those whose hope is for music to somehow "transcend" its original boundaries. One understands even the commercial motivation of those who feel the urge to find "contemporary" (and sometimes provocative) ways to present certain repertoire that they fear may be showing its age. But particularly with compositions that are closely identified with war victims, ethnicity, and religion, the motivation that should transcend all others is *respect*—in this case for the composer's own spiritual motivation, and for those listeners whose personal convictions mirror this motivation. Just as Americans take great care to be respectful of their neighbors' religious icons, they should be just as careful and respectful of *musical rep-*

resentations of these very same icons. Failure to do so can betray not just shockingly poor taste, but can be deeply offensive and hurtful to those who cherish these manifestations of religious conviction.

The earlier hypothetical examples and the actual performance in question go beyond insensitivity. They enter the realm of sacrilege, which is defined as "the desecration, profanation, misuse, or theft of something sacred." Are there any words more sacred to Christians than Jesus' final utterances from the Cross? For these believers, what music could possibly be more sacred than music that is specifically based on these words? Unlike generally "spiritual" music that can suit various occasions, music whose identity and integrity are derived from its umbilical-like connection to a sacred text is not just misused, but is desecrated and profaned when this life-sustaining connection is severed, then reattached to something altogether foreign. Like Siamese twins who share the same vital organs, sacred music and the sacred texts upon which it is based cannot be separated from each other without risking serious harm to one, the other, or both.

In many instances, professional musicians and concert presenters who abuse sacred music may simply be unaware of the depth of the offense they cause, oblivious to the consequences of their own shallow zeal. If their transgression stems from ignorance rather than intent, offended persons might respond by taking a cue from the second movement of Haydn's Good Friday masterpiece and "forgive them for they know not what they do." But in this case there is little doubt that everyone involved was well aware what they were doing, as demonstrated by the poet's comments that were printed in the concert program. "I'm a nonbeliever in anything religious. . . . A nonreligious person takes on a religious theme, and how does he go about it? Does he accept the religious premise of the seven last words? Or does he reject the premise and supply his own terms? . . . I didn't use the words Jesus or God because then you get into clichés. The Gospels have become such a cliché, such an often-told tale that it doesn't allow for much originality. I didn't want to subscribe to the idea of Christ as a man who goes around working miracles. I think this is a primitive form of publicity for the new religion . . . God, I can't write about this divine stuff, I don't believe in magic!"

One would never replace the Cross in a Catholic Church with another object, such as the three-pointed corporate logo of Mercedes-Benz. Though the Mercedes symbol is inoffensive (to Christians too) in virtually any other context, few would disagree that such an act would be outrageous. If the same test were applied to the Star of David at a Jewish synagogue, or to the design on the prayer rug in a Muslim mosque, it is again clear that these are extremely offensive hypothetical examples of sacrilege. By the same token, one should never do something, encourage something, or facilitate something that could give the impression to "the faithful" (who are naturally the ones most likely to be sensitive) that one is tampering with *musical* expressions of their religious conviction.

In the immediate aftermath of that particular Haydn performance— a sacrilegious musical offering if ever there was one—I rationalized that it had clarified, at least, some very important boundaries. But as I now recall the poet's still-shocking comments, comments that reveal the very worst strain of sacrilege—that which is informed and deliberate—I see in Raymond Brown's "forgiveness" meditation a suggested response that moves away from righteous indignation toward temperance and reconciliation. After discussing Luke's unique view of Jesus which emphasizes the "healing, forgiving, reconciling ministry that filled his public life," Father Brown asks, "should *we* not be challenged to go further and forgive even those who *do* know the wrong that they are doing?"

SYMBOLS OF CHANGE

The preaching tradition in black churches is unlike any other. Over the years we have heard some of the very best at Rockefeller Chapel, including Edgar Thornton, B. Herbert Martin, Jeremiah Wright, Donald Parson, James Meeks, and of course T. L. Barrett. There is an extroverted, freewheeling, and uninhibited quality to their styles, the consequences of which can be not just rousing but spellbinding. In black churches there is also a traditional role for the congregation, altogether different from that in mostly-white churches. The members of the congregation jump in. They let loose, unhesitatingly and often loudly. They interact with the pastor, with the choir, with other members of the congregation. Because they feed off each other's energy, there is an infectious sense of exuberant liberation. Similar to the way an inspired jazz musician will improvise within a predetermined progression of chords, their behavior can be spontaneous but not entirely unpredictable or undisciplined, as hinted by a line from a collection of black church music: "Spontaneity does not necessarily mean lack of rehearsal."[10] It is therefore different only in style from the guiding principles of Earle Brown's *Available Forms*. It has not been so easy to import this wonderful spirit into Rockefeller's austere environment, but when it has happened the results have been awesome.

The ordination of women is a frequently discussed issue in the Catholic Church. Many articulate and passionate voices on both sides, within and outside the Church, have provided much food for thought for Catholics and non-Catholics alike. For some reason there has not been as vigorous a debate regarding the role of women in top positions of authority in African-American churches. While we see more and more female clergy members in black churches, it is uncommon to see women in senior pastor positions.

Gifted African-American women are managing to gradually break down these invisible barriers, thanks in part to some extraordinary pioneers, one of whom is Rev. Addie Wyatt, who joined us at Rockefeller in 2002. As described in her bio, Addie was a trailblazer not just for black women but for *all* women. Though she is now advanced in years and needs help getting around, she still exudes a charisma and an aura that commands both respect and love. Reading the text of her meditation does not fully enable one to experience the power of her personality. Never forced, never hurried, her heart "sang" to us, and in so doing it lovingly opened *our* hearts. But more than that, she reminded us that those who hold others back—intentionally or not, on the national stage or closer to home—are more likely to be sensitive to messages of change if the messengers are not only as persuasive but also as benevolent as Addie Wyatt, as illustrated by her beautiful meditation on *"Father, forgive them, for they know not what they do."*

Just as Rev. Wyatt helped create opportunities for millions of American women throughout the last half of the twentieth century, she also paved the way on a more modest scale for the appearance of Rev. Yvonne Hawkins at Rockefeller in 2003. I had heard Yvonne a year earlier at the Congregational Church of Park Manor at a Good Friday service which featured sermons by several prominent black pastors from Chicago's South Side. Listed as an assistant pastor at Park Manor Christian Church, Rev. Hawkins was the only woman among them. While the other speakers were excellent, Yvonne was riveting.

She made much the same impression at Rockefeller. Her style was a mixture of colloquial and mainstream rhetoric, of soothing warmth and what kids now call "attitude." She could sound both like your loving big sister and a street-smart "sister." Especially impressive to me was that she was so very "musical" in her vocal inflection, in her unerring instincts for timing and pacing, and in her exploitation of distinctive rhythmic patterns.

> It doesn't matter who your mama was.
> It doesn't matter who your daddy was.
> It doesn't matter how many brothers or sisters you had.
> It doesn't even matter if you grew up on the wrong side
>   of the tracks.
> None of that matters.
> When the nitty hit the gritty, the *only* thing that mattered
>   was that each thief had an opportunity.
> And to the one who took it, Jesus said,
> *"Today you will be with me in paradise."*

Though the flavor is altogether different, the language is similar to "John's rhythmic, meditative, iconic account of the death of Jesus," to which Dr. David Tracy refers in his brilliant meditation on *"I thirst."* This topic is addressed in detail by the theologian Amos N. Wilder, the brother of the famous playwright. In his analysis of the First Epistle of John, Wilder focuses on "verse-forms," "recurrent features of balanced phrasing," and examples of "rhetorical prose"[11] which are unique to John. Compare the following illustrations with the distinctive rhetorical style that Yvonne Hawkins and other black preachers so frequently employ.

That which was from the beginning,
  which we have heard,
  which we have seen with our eyes,
  which we have looked upon
  and touched with our hands. (1 John 1:1)

I am writing to you, little children . . .
I am writing to you, fathers . . .
I am writing to you, young men . . . (1 John 2:12)

This discussion is related to Haydn's use of recurring rhythmic and melodic fragments *(motives)*, particularly in his musical representations of *"I thirst"* and *"It is finished!"*—movements which, not coincidentally, are based on the Gospel of John. It is true that *motivic development* is a common compositional technique that composers have relied on for centuries. But is it coincidental that Haydn's particular use of distinctive strands of rhythmic and melodic "DNA" not only contributes to this music's inherent unity and integrity, but is essential to its virtually perfect balance and proportion? [See the analysis of *"I thirst"* and *"It is finished!"* in "The Words and the Music."] This is a question that is impossible for us to answer since it is one of many secrets Haydn took to his grave. But like so many other queries that may occur to us in the course of this journey, the mere *asking* of the question is exhilarating and enlightening.

The response of the Rockefeller audience to Yvonne Hawkins' preaching was thrilling. Even a few white folks in those old wooden pews found themselves mouthing "Amen!" and "Praise the Lord!" along with the more vocal black audience members seated in their midst. I smiled as I recalled that long ago letter from "a loyal listener" who complained about "the appropriateness of the speaker."

GOOD FRIDAY DISCOMFORTS

Martin Marty said to me once, "Good Friday is not about being comfortable." There is no doubt that this pilgrimage has provided more than a few uncomfortable bumps in the road. One of the most memorable is Rev. Gregory Dell's brilliant 2000 meditation on *"Woman, behold your son!" "Behold your mother!"* which challenged certain "traditional" attitudes toward gays. A similar theme is beautifully embedded in the meditation on *"I thirst"* by Rev. Dorothy McRae-McMahon. She is one of seven prominent members of the Australian clergy who participated in our *Seven Last Words* performances in Sydney, Melbourne, Canberra, Adelaide, and Perth in 1997. Heavy with private pathos yet buoyed by inspired prose that is so gracefully balanced, her meditation was conceived as she was being pressured to resign from her church in the wake of her public declaration that she is gay.

In 1999 Rev. Seiichi Michael Yasutake delivered a forceful and eloquent meditation on *"Father, forgive them, for they know not what they do."* He was a rather small and elegant elderly man, and his words were spoken with quiet measured intensity. What makes his message resonate with surprising power can be found in the fine print of his biography. Rev. Yasutake had been one of thousands of Japanese Americans illegally imprisoned by the United States government in internment camps during World War II. Such a man has earned the right to speak to us about the significance of forgiveness.

In recent years Father Michael Pfleger has been a lightning rod for controversy in the Catholic Church because of his very critical comments regarding racism directed not only toward whites, but also toward the Church itself. No one can question Father Mike's sincerity, his intelligence, or his religious conviction. Moreover his efforts have brought about many positive changes in the lives of his parishioners. But he is an agitator, a conscience-disturber who can make people very uncomfortable, particularly other white Catholics. He forces his listeners to look at themselves in the mirror and come to grips with who they really are and what they really stand for.

The presence of a prominent Mormon, Elder Dallin Oaks, on our recording has caused a considerable amount of discomfort among certain Christians. Given the history of tension between the church of Latter-day Saints and some Christian groups, I cannot say I was entirely surprised. Nevertheless, I was caught off guard by those manifestations of discomfort where the line that separates fundamental philosophical disagreement from religious intolerance was not so clearly drawn. I was also sobered by the realization that the face of intolerance may sometimes be a familiar and friendly one. Perhaps the most appropriate response is one that avoids the temptation to differentiate and feels no compulsion to judge or justify: "If anyone hears my words and does not believe, I do not judge him; for I did not come to judge the world but to save the world." (John 12:47)

GOOD FRIDAY GRACE

A memorable incident occurred at downtown Chicago's Fourth Presbyterian Church in 1994 even before the actual performance began. It was about an hour before we were scheduled to start. We had just finished a brief rehearsal with Rev. John Buchanan and a few early arrivals had begun to trickle in. I had left my viola in the office that we were using as our dressing room, and decided to look for a water fountain in the foyer. As I proceeded through the sanctuary I was approached by a rather strange looking fellow.

I cannot tell you his age—he could have been anywhere between thirty and fifty. In any event, he clearly had the look of a homeless person, though he was clean and I could see that he had taken some trouble with his appearance. He had shaved (though with apparent difficulty), his worn shoes had a nice new shine, and he was wearing a brand-new pair of jeans and a bright white sweatshirt with bold lettering on the front that read, "PROUD TO BE AN AMERICAN." He said to me, "I want to thank you for coming here to play this piece tonight. It means an awful lot to me." I thanked him and started to leave when he got even closer, almost right up in my face. With his voice beginning to quiver, he said, "I don't think you understand. Things have been difficult for me recently. But I believe that years from now I'll be able to look back on this performance and know that *this* is what enabled me to turn my life around."

Throughout the performance I could see him out of the corner of my eye. He was sitting in the very front row, listening the way you wish everyone would listen: hanging on every word, every note, every silence. He was the first to jump to his feet at the conclusion of *The Earthquake*, tears streaking his cheeks, applauding vigorously.

I have thought about that fellow many times since. He is someone you would never see at a subscription concert by a major symphony orchestra, at a Metropolitan Opera performance, or at one of our regular Vermeer Quartet concerts. Yet because of what *this* piece represents, he had come to Fourth Presbyterian Church to hear us. And I felt honored by his presence. For here was the essence, revealed through an anonymous fellow drifter, of what Haydn had meant when he expressed the hope "that even the most uninitiated listener will be moved to the very depths of his soul." I don't think I have ever felt a greater responsibility to play my very best.

Father Richard Neuhaus has written of "the aura of redemptive suffering, of suffering 'offered up' on behalf of others."[12] This "aura," so germane to the crucifixion of Jesus, was never more present at our *Seven Last Words* performances than during Stan Guthrie's penetrating *"I thirst"* at Rockefeller in April 2000. What made these words so poignant was that they were delivered by a man whose own body had been crippled and bent by cerebral palsy. With Father Greeley helping him to the pulpit, Stan spoke with simple sincerity and without a trace of self-pity: "Jesus was not a spirit trapped in a shell. He was a perfect man with an imperfect body, and now, before the Resurrection, his body betrayed him. How like us! Jesus knew firsthand the frustration, the agony of the physical."

That was not the only drama of the evening involving Stan Guthrie. A passionate evangelical, he was uncomfortable appearing on the same program with Rev. Gregory Dell, the Methodist pastor who had drawn international attention for having performed a "ceremony of holy union" between two gay men. Stan worried that his participation with Dell might appear to be a tacit endorsement of something altogether foreign to *his* Christian beliefs. I reminded Stan that these presentations (indeed Jesus' message) draw strength from the diversity of the messengers, whose individual perspectives reflect in sometimes very different ways Jesus' example of love and grace. Are not one's convictions fortified, rather than diminished, whenever they are appropriately tested? The answer came a week or so later when, after much introspection, Stan graciously accepted my invitation.

That night prior to the performance I observed Stan Guthrie and Gregory Dell, two very good men, huddled together in quiet conversation. They were engaged in more than polite chatter as they listened to each other, *really* listened, in a manner that I wish others could more often do. Later that evening their meditations seemed to blend and bleed into one another: "The word of Christ at the moment of his greatest agony was a radical word of love and grace," [Dell]. "Suspended between heaven and earth, he has shown us how we should respond as we await our own resurrection," [Guthrie].

Finally I wish to share one of this journey's most heart-wrenching experiences. It happened at Rockefeller in 1998. A friend of mine, Celeste Bedard, was dying from an inoperable brain tumor, and I am convinced she willed herself to stay alive long enough to attend the performance. A vibrant young woman in her late twenties, I had met her at the People's Music School where I do inner-city volunteer work. She had recently attended two of our other Vermeer Quartet concerts in Chicago, including a benefit for the Make-a-Wish Foundation. But *The Seven Last Words of Christ* was the one that meant the most to her, in part because of the private hours she had spent listening to our CD.

It was a magnificent group of speakers that year, and I told her I would try to arrange introductions, particularly with Francis Cardinal George since Celeste was Catholic. All the speakers knew about her situation—Alison Boden even inserted the word "celestial" in her meditation—and they stayed to greet her afterwards. Andrew Greeley was first. He walked right up to her wheelchair, bent down and said without hesitation, "I love you, Celeste." Then came the others: Martin Marty, Jean Elshtain, Alison Boden, Dick Staub, B. Herbert Martin, Samuel Betances, and John Buchanan. Finally, Cardinal George blessed her and prayed with her for a few priceless minutes as the rest of us stood off to the side brushing back tears.

As emotional as that was, the most poignant moments of the evening may already have occurred during two of the meditations—with Celeste, her parents, and her twin sister (imagine!) listening from the back of the darkened chapel. The first, from John Buchanan's highly personal *"Woman, behold your son!" "Behold your mother!":* "Parents should not experience the death of their children. Everything about that is wrong, out of sync. Children are supposed to bury their parents, not the other way around." The second, from Andrew Greeley's concluding meditation: "The seven last words of Jesus are also *our* seven last words—the words of terror and loneliness, of fear and horror, of despair and final surrender as we complete our journey and perhaps begin a new one. Yet they are not words without hope. On Good Friday we ask whether we can face death with hope, even as Jesus did when he said, *'Father, into your hands I commend my spirit.'"*

Though Father Greeley had written these words weeks before he learned of Celeste's grave condition, it was as if he had intended them just for her. Thank God she was able to hear them in time! She died a short time later.

COMING FULL CIRCLE

As the story about Gertrude Stein suggests, the questions one asks during a journey may be as important as the answers found at journey's end. At this point I think I understand many of the answers, but I still don't always know how to arrive at them. So for now, an altered version of Peter Gomes' earlier metaphor fits well. *I know where I am. And I know where I want to go. I just don't always know how I'm going to get there.* But if the key is to learn which questions to ask and how to better ask them, these Seven Last Words meditations may well provide an effective means to the end. And perhaps they can also be useful to others who are involved in similar pilgrimages—those who are not too busy, too confident, or too proud to "ask for directions." It is largely because these reflections are often so intensely personal—like the bond between a parent and a child—that one can embrace them with such conviction.

In 1785, the same year a Spanish bishop approached Haydn to write *The Seven Last Words of Christ,* the music world's newest young sensation, Wolfgang Amadeus Mozart, published a set of six string quartets that he dedicated to Haydn. Mozart felt not only indebted to his mentor, but so personally invested in these six quartets that he wrote the following words in the dedication.

To my dear friend Haydn: A father who had decided to send his children into the world at large thought best to entrust them to the protection and guidance of a famous man who fortunately happened to be his best friend as well. Behold here, famous man and dearest friend, my six children.

[Into your hands I entrust . . . Father, behold your son. Behold your son's children.]

My feelings for many of these Seven Last Words meditations are similar to Mozart's feelings for his six "children." But whereas Haydn was so overwhelmed by the young Mozart's genius that he didn't complete a single string quartet in the last ten years of his life, these meditations have inspired me to explore avenues that I might otherwise have overlooked. I suspect that they will awaken similar feelings in others, and that they too, in turn, will "entrust them to the protection and guidance" of others. Many readers will draw strength from the meditations in the way that an observer draws inspiration from a painting. But more than that, they will gravitate to them in the way that people who are "drawn into the drama" become participants. But here rather than a micro-drama—"a play within a play," like Ruggiero Leoncavallo's *Pagliacci* or Archibald Macleish's *J.B.*—we have a macro-drama: "a play beyond the play," in which we become participants in something of far greater significance. And because we are now part of it, we are able to personally identify with this macro-drama. All this is possible because, as Andrew Greeley points out in his introduction, "the seven last words of Jesus are also the seven last words of all of *us*, and of the God who suffers with us."

As impressive as these meditations are by themselves, they are even more compelling when heard in the company of Franz Joseph Haydn's music. For all great music has an indefinable aura that not only allows it to transcend its own acoustical properties and "spiritual" core, but enables its accompanying words to be fortified with new insight and to resonate with unexpected urgency. More than that, music—particularly when tethered to persuasive words—is uniquely empowering. Leo Tolstoy wrote:

Music makes me forget myself, my own reality. It transports me to some other place far from my everyday existence. Under music's influence it seems that I can feel what I normally could not feel, that I understand what I would not otherwise understand, that I can do what I could never do.[13]

Music can speak to us, each one of us, with its own distinctive voice in its own special language—not just this particular music of Haydn but, in a larger sense, *music* the metaphor: "At night, when worries sleep and the city is hiding in the dark, oh how much music there is with God, what sounds there are on earth!"[14] *Music* illuminates significant words by providing additional layers of texture that both sharpen and soften their meaning, as needed. It allows us to better balance the competing voices of our minds and hearts. Even more important, *music* puts those who "listen" in closer contact with words' larger context and deeper meaning. And if *holy* words bring us closer to God, does not their accompanying music bring us yet closer?

Meanwhile there are some who enjoy hearing Haydn's music, but are more comfortable listening to *the music* from a discrete distance. Their skepticism compels them to maintain "a certain objective curiosity." For them, the following passage by Dylan Thomas may be useful.

I read somewhere of a shepherd who, when asked why he made, from within fairy rings, ritual observances to the moon to protect his flocks, replied: "I'd be a damn' fool if I didn't!" These poems, with all their crudities, doubts, and confusions, are written for the love of Man and in praise of God, and I'd be a damn' fool if they weren't.[15]

THE
INTRODUCTION

T. L. BARRETT

It is impossible to separate this wonderful music by Haydn from the religious focus that served as its inspiration. It was, after all, conceived as an integral part of a Good Friday service, and to divorce the music—however powerfully it stands alone—from the context for which it was originally intended is to hear it in only part of its glory.

Let me now summarize the seven most important events that immediately preceded Jesus' seven final utterances.

1. The greatest meal in history . . . the Last Supper of Jesus with his disciples.
2. The greatest period of anticipation in history . . . experienced by Jesus in the Garden of Gethsemane when he asked his disciples to wait with him for one agonizing hour.
3. The greatest act of betrayal in history . . . when Jesus was betrayed by Judas for a mere thirty pieces of silver.
4. The greatest mockery of justice in history . . . the trial of Jesus before Pontius Pilate.
5. The greatest burden ever placed on the shoulders of one person . . . when Jesus was forced to carry his cross up the hill to Calvary.
6. The greatest act of cowardice in history . . . the desertion at the Cross of all but one of Jesus' disciples.
7. The greatest suffering ever experienced by any man or woman . . . when Jesus was nailed to the Cross and left to die.

Here now are the seven greatest final words in history . . . words that continue to resonate to this very day . . . *The Seven Last Words of Christ.*

ANDREW M. GREELEY

Good Friday is the day of the triumph of evil. Goodness, perhaps ultimate goodness, is tormented and destroyed. An innocent man dies a terrible death, one among many innocents who have died terrible deaths even to this day, but a special good man who represented in a unique way the goodness of God. How could God permit this to happen, we wonder? If God were really this man's parent, he must be a very poor parent. For what kind of parent would permit this to happen to a beloved son if he could prevent it? Good Friday is the day of all days when the problem of evil is most poignantly posed. Is God either a monster or not God?

Annie Dillard suggests that perhaps God cannot be blamed:

> God is no more blinding people with glaucoma, or testing them with diabetes, or purifying them with spinal pain, or choreographing the seeding of tumor cells through lymph, or fiddling chromosomes than he is jimmying floodwaters or pitching tornadoes at towns. God is no more cogitating which among us he plans to place here as bird-headed dwarfs or elephant men—or to kill by AIDS or kidney failure, heart disease, childhood leukemia or sudden infant death syndrome—than he is pitching lightening bolts at pedestrians, triggering rock slides, or setting fires.

The lesson of Good Friday is that God suffers with us. Like every good parent he suffers when his children suffer. When Jesus hung from the Cross, God made common cause with the Albanian peasant shot in the back of the head and tossed into a pit to be consumed by fire. God cannot prevent our suffering, but he suffers with us. When the little baby cries, Berdyaev the Russian mystic wrote, God weeps.

How can this be? How can God suffer? Isn't God above all suffering? One can only reply that the God of the Hebrew scriptures presents himself as suffering with his people. No Greek philosophy can refute that. Moreover Good Friday is good precisely because God on that day identified himself with the sufferings of his people.

Dillard again:

Nature works out its complexities. God suffers the world's necessities along with us, suffers our turning away, and joins us in exile. Christians might add that Christ hangs, as it were, on the Cross forever, always incarnate and always nailed.

The Catholic crucifix is the symbol of the ongoing suffering of God with us. The seven last words of Jesus are also the seven last words of all of us, and of the God who suffers with us.

LYDIA TALBOT

A story that began heralding a way through the wilderness now ends on the way to the cross, not the religious icon, but the ultimate deterrent to those who would challenge the sovereignty of Rome. For Jesus, it was the most inhumane form of capital punishment: execution by crucifixion.

Consider the scandal of Good Friday as a headline report on the nightly news, inspired by theologian Robert McAfee Brown.

Leading the news this Friday evening. . . . The insurgency movement led by a young Galilean peasant came to an end today after a weeklong uprising that began last Sunday. Jesus of Nazareth was executed on a dump heap outside the city wall. It has been a week full of intrigue, as authorities tried to contain a movement that increasingly threatened them as the week went on. Each day the leader of the insurgents challenged both religious and political establishments in a series of explosive encounters. On Monday, temple police were summoned when Jesus angrily upset tables on money-changers and went after them with a whip, claiming they had "turned a house of prayer into a den of robbers."

All week there have been brisk encounters and heckling in the streets. Jesus allegedly challenged the authority of Caesar by urging people not to give Caesar what should only be given to God. By Wednesday evening, it appeared authorities were plotting to kill him. After his group had celebrated the Passover meal on Thursday evening, they went to the Mount of Olives, where soldiers were already waiting to arrest Jesus. Unconfirmed reports claim that one of his members named Judas defected with intelligence that made the arrest almost routine.

By sun-up, it was determined that Jesus was a threat to Caesar. He was beaten with billy clubs by local police, bound and brought before Pontius Pilate, who disposed of the matter by washing his hands and allowing a raging mob to sentence Jesus to death. Soldiers stripped him naked, draped a scarlet robe around him, then set a crown of thorns on his head. They thrust a staff in his right hand, knelt in front of him, mocked him, spat upon him, bludgeoned him repeatedly on the head with the staff, and forced him to carry his own stake to be crucified with two criminals. Deserted by all but one of his followers, he was nailed to the cross with spikes driven through his hands and feet. Reliable witnesses observed a sudden darkness for three hours and a turbulent earthquake that struck when Jesus died at the Place of the Skull. His followers have temporarily gone into hiding.

Now, these reports just in from three experts with differing views of the events. . . . The head of Roman security forces maintains they could not apprehend Jesus publicly without incurring negative approval. Some of their smartest operatives asked him sophisticated questions in front of large crowds, but after the blasphemy of suggesting that his God was greater than Caesar, they infiltrated his group and performed a clean and efficient operation without resistance. The official says Jerusalem will be a safer place without Jesus.

One organizer for the homeless in Jerusalem reports a different assessment of Jesus. She says his message gave the common people great hope; he was preaching "good news to the poor and liberty to the captives." He was not an "expert on the problems of poor people"; he was poor himself. By his own admission, he had "nowhere to lay his head." The homeless had hoped that he would be the one to save them.

43

Describing some of the teachings of Jesus, one of his followers named Bartholomew says that it all comes down to the need to love one another. It is not easy to do, but he says Jesus promised that if we keep on trying, God will give us the power to do a better job. Jesus wanted people to work together instead of competing against each other. That means sharing our goods, freeing prisoners, and canceling our debts. He really believed that everybody could change—rich, poor, men, women, children, elderly, straight, gay, black, brown, yellow, white—all could be part of a new sort of family. Bartholomew recalls that Jesus had said that if he died, God would raise him from the dead, not just in the hearts of his people, but maybe in some other ways as well. He also suggested that whatever happens, Jesus' story will not have ended at three o'clock this afternoon.

We return now to those final agonizing hours of endurance, when a suffering Jesus, stretched out on the Cross in excruciating pain, uttered his last words: *The Seven Last Words of Christ.*

JOHN SHEA

Christians do more than listen to the words of Jesus. They meditate on them, pulling them into their hearts and feasting on their many meanings. They do this because they believe with St. John the Evangelist that the One Eternal Word spoke through the many words of Jesus.

St. John writes, "In the beginning was the Word, and the Word was with God, and the Word was God." This suggests there was always a Word coming forth. There was never a self-contained God. There was always an unfolding. There was never an isolated glory. There was always an inner fullness spilling over, like a wedding with too much wine, like a net with too many fish, like the slow, thick fall of perfume from an alabaster vase, its fragrance filling the whole world. As it flowed, it created.

So St. John continues, "All things were made through the Word. There was nothing that was made that was *not* made through the Word." His vision is that through this Word the cosmos is intricately built up, nesting layer within layer, spiraling, weaving, generating, pulsing. All that was, is, and will be hums with the life of this Word.

And then, St. John takes a bold step. He tells us this "Word became flesh." It entered into a man, dwelt in him with a fullness that was ripe and bursting like a tree that could bear fruit in any season. This One Word broke into the many words of human speech, like a man would take one loaf of bread and, breaking it, offer it to all. So in this man the One Word became many words, hoping we could hear its offer of life in the voice of one like us. That is why Christians meditate on the words of Christ. They desire the life that sustains and transforms all there is.

According to the Gospel, Jesus once took disciples and went up a mountain. There, his inner being blazed forth, making his face radiant and his garments white. The disciples wanted to build a tent. But a cloud descended, and a voice from the cloud urged another response. "This is my beloved Son in whom I am well pleased," the voice said. "Listen to him." Do not build a tent. Open your ears.

So let us listen to him as he forgives the ignorance of his executioners. Let us listen to him as he promises paradise to a common criminal, his crucified partner. Let us listen to him as he encourages a woman to behold a new son, and a son to behold a new mother. Let us listen to him as he cries to God for an explanation of his abandonment. Let us listen to him as he reveals the core of his being as a thirst. Let us listen to him as he sighs and finishes what he has begun. Let us listen to him as he surrenders his spirit into invisible hands. Let us listen to the Last Words of the man in whom the One Word Became Many Words: The Seven Last Words of Christ.

ALLAN B. WARREN

Dictatorships are always brutal, and a military government can be seen as little more than organized crime claiming legitimacy. Imperial Rome. Hitler's Germany. From one perspective there is not much difference. But, of course, beneath the surface there is insecurity, and whatever is not controlled is perceived to be a threat—even an itinerant rabbi with a small following.

The Gospels give no indication that Jesus ever challenged Rome and its power. Indeed, when asked about paying taxes, did he not reply, "Render unto Caesar . . ." His quarrel seems to have been mainly with the establishment of his own religion . . . an establishment also insecure, keen to placate the Roman conquerors and hold on to its own power and prestige, however tenuous.

"You have heard it said . . . but I say to you." Who does this man think he is? "Destroy this temple and in three days I will raise it up." The son of a carpenter—we know his parents and his background—how can he make such claims? This is blasphemy. He is a fraud. This is dangerous.

And so they tried him in their own courts, and then they took him to Pilate, the military governor, who had the power of death. We know from the Gospels and also from sources outside them, that Pilate was a fairly sorry sort of man. Embittered. His career had not been a success, and here he was stuck in Palestine, an unpleasant place populated by religious fanatics. He hated it. And so, don't let anyone rock the boat, put them down—for Pilate that was the way to handle things.

Therefore, when the leaders came to him and the mob assembled, he gave them what they wanted. Crucify him? Why not? What's the harm? Who knows, maybe he is dangerous. Besides, one less zealot—can't hurt.

And so they beat him, and when they finished, the soldiers had a little fun. Thorns wrapped around his head for a crown to match Pilate's sign, "The King of the Jews." And they gave him a reed for a scepter, put a robe on him, and bowed down. And then they laughed at him and spit in his face. When their sport was over, they made him drag his cross through the city and up the hill. They nailed him to it. Stood it up. He hung there until he died. There were a few people with him. Most, however, had fled. Only his mother, a few women, and one disciple (out of twelve) were brave enough to stay beside him.

The Gospels record Jesus' speaking seven times as he died. And what a contrast are his words of courage and faith to the obscene spectacle of his betrayal. For centuries the Church has pondered the meaning of those words. Here now are meditations upon them.

MARTIN E. MARTY

"Jesus will be in agony even to the end of the world. We must not sleep in that time . . ." So wrote the great mathematician and philosopher Pascal. He believed that this crucified Jesus had risen from the dead. But he also pictured Jesus always in agony in the middle of the world.

Wherever anyone is in agony, anyone suffers, anyone is denied love, anyone is cut off from justice, anywhere in the world, to the eye of the person of faith, Jesus is in agony. Agony: "intense pain of mind or body"; agony: "the struggle that precedes death"; agony: a reality one would like to escape; agony: it forces itself upon anyone who reflects on Jesus and his Cross. Four Gospel writers capture seven words from Jesus in agony. They are words that stab the hearts of millions on the bad day that people call Good Friday. Agony: this is an ugliness that cannot be obscured even when the beauty of Haydn's music colors it.

Through the centuries believers have figuratively stood at the foot of the Cross and pondered the agony of Jesus. During these long ages there has been time for many to overwork their imaginations. Thus some describe Jesus' agony as the most intense pain of body anyone ever suffered. They have bequeathed carved statues and stained glass pictures of Jesus in such pain, to stimulate a sense of guilt or profound sympathy among those who remember him, who love him.

Must faith focus on that intensity of physical pain? True, it is hard to picture worse misery than that which comes with crucifixion. There is pain of choking, of exposure, of contortion, of wounds open. Yet comparative pain analysis was never the best approach to the Gospel story. Tonight, in many places in the world, fiends torture innocents, using their perverted imaginations to inflict the worst kind of pain. Tonight, even in healing places such as in clinics only hundreds of yards from here, agents of mercy work to lessen the pain of some who suffer unimaginably. Many sufferers withstand torture or stand pain by identifying themselves in their agony with Jesus in his. So his seven words, spoken in agony, breathe comforting spirit in their ears, to their souls.

Agony is also "intense pain of mind . . ." In this second case, the disciples did and believers do think of Jesus' agony as the most profound ever. For in the stories that issue from this Friday event come sets of meanings that say Jesus suffered for others; that he carried their burdens and the weight of their wrongs; that he was an example of love and justice in the company of people who were denied both before, during, and after the Friday we identify with these seven words.

While Jesus is in agony, "we must not sleep . . ." said Pascal. It is easy to misinterpret that urging word. Hours before Jesus' death his closest friends and disciples, understandably weary, had fallen asleep as he prayed. They left him alone in agony, as we are told not to do. Yet in the new creation that has come after he conquered death, those who follow Jesus also know that he does not only rouse his followers to restless and selfless action. He also brings the blessings of rest and peace.

But that peace must wait, for now, while he speaks and we hear those seven utterances from the Cross: The Seven Last Words of Christ.

Richard Young

Jesus spoke his *seven last words* under the most desperate circumstances—after he'd been nailed to a cross and left to die. Only the most faithful could then have believed the promise of what was to follow: the raising of Jesus from the dead—the Resurrection.

Many believed Jesus to be the Christ—the son of God and savior of mankind. He was therefore a threat to those in power. He predicted that he would suffer and die at their hands, but would be raised from the dead by God three days later. He anticipated that someone close to him would betray him, and that others would eventually desert him. After sharing the Last Supper with his disciples, Jesus was arrested in the Garden of Gethsemane, where he had gone to pray. It was one of his most devoted followers (Judas!) who had betrayed him.

He was brought before the governor, Pontius Pilate, who conveniently *washed his hands of the matter* by allowing the volatile crowd to determine Jesus' fate. Mob justice prevailed, and they demanded that Jesus be put to death, using the most painfully cruel method of execution known to man. The soldiers stripped him naked, they draped a scarlet robe around him, and attached a crown of razor-sharp thorns to his head. They ridiculed him, they spat on him, they savagely beat him, before finally dragging him away to be crucified with two common thieves. Jesus was forced to carry his own cross up the hill to the killing area at Calvary—a location appropriately known as *the place of the skull.* Deserted by all but one of his disciples, he was nailed to the Cross—spikes driven through his hands and feet!—and he suffered a prolonged and excruciating death. A tremendous earthquake immediately followed.

Jesus' body was taken down from the Cross and sealed in a tomb. But three days later, it was discovered that the huge stone which closed off the tomb's entrance had somehow been moved away, and the body had vanished. Matthew writes that an angel appeared and announced that Jesus (as promised) had risen from the dead. To his enraptured followers, there was no doubt that the Resurrection had indeed taken place. The prophecy had been fulfilled. And as a result, the lives of countless believers, then and now, had been graced with special meaning.

Let's return now to those torturous final hours when Jesus was hanging from the Cross—life being drained from him, moment by agonizing moment. Despite the intense pain, despite the humiliation, despite the overwhelming despair of having been so utterly betrayed and abandoned, he was somehow at peace—his judgment *more sure*, his inspiration *more vivid*, his faith *more profound* than ever! It was in these moments of ultimate physical torment and spiritual ecstasy that he uttered his final, fateful words: *The Seven Last Words of Christ!*

When they had come to
the place called Calvary,
there they crucified him
along with the criminals, one
on the right hand and the other
on the left. Then Jesus said,

"FATHER, FORGIVE THEM,
FOR THEY KNOW NOT
WHAT THEY DO."

LUKE 23:34

"FATHER, FORGIVE THEM, FOR THEY KNOW NOT WHAT THEY DO."

VIRGIL P. ELIZONDO

From the throne of his cathedral, Jesus proclaimed the most beautiful and powerful word of life. In a world poisoned and torn apart by violence, vengeance, betrayals, abandonment, insults, and indifference, forgiveness is the only way to inner freedom, peace, and tranquility. Without forgiveness, life is worse than death, and death is eternal torment.

Jesus lived in such a world. He was betrayed, abused, and abandoned. Yet he lived to forgive. For only in forgiveness is even death dissolved into life everlasting, and previous pains transformed into unending joy. To forgive is to live.

RAYMOND E. BROWN

The Italian poet Dante described Luke as *scriba mansuetudinis Christi,* the evangelist who described for us the sweet gentleness of Christ. Nowhere is that more evident than in the three words that the crucified Jesus speaks in Luke's Gospel, of which this is the first. In Luke's view, the Jesus of the Passion narrative continues the healing, forgiving, reconciling ministry that filled his public life.

Only in Luke's passion does Jesus heal the ear of the servant who came to the Mount of Olives to arrest him. Only in Luke does Jesus reconcile Herod and Pilate, his judges who had been enemies up to the time they met him. Only in Luke does Jesus stop on the way to the Cross to express his concern about the Daughters of Jerusalem who wept for him. And only in Luke will he extend his grace to the criminal crucified with him who asked to be remembered. And so it is not surprising that again, only in Luke, do we have from the crucified Jesus a word like *"Father, forgive them. They do not know what they are doing."*

In loyalty to a Lucan Jesus who told of the mercy of the father for the prodigal son, should *we* not be challenged to go further and forgive even those who *do* know the wrong that they are doing?

DON WYCLIFF

An innocent man stands condemned. His name is Jesus. His name is Anthony Porter. His name is Rolando Cruz. His name is that of any of the more than a hundred men who have been released from Death Rows or maximum-security cellblocks after the miracle of DNA proved their innocence. His name might be that of any of the several hundred men—and women—who have *not* been released, but whose passage through the "justice" system ended—as Jesus' ended—in ignominious death.

To be innocent and yet condemned to die as a criminal—whether on a cross or on a gurney with arm outstretched to receive the lethal needle—is awful enough. But to be innocent and yet found guilty at trial—that may be even more nightmarish.

Of course, Jesus knew what sort of an exercise his trial was. He maintained his silence because he knew he was going to be found guilty no matter what the facts of the case might be. This was not an exercise in truth-seeking, but a political proceeding to rid the community of a dangerous disturber of the peace and a challenger of the established order.

But the innocent-yet-condemned men of our time . . . their predicaments result from our society's most highly ritualized exercise in truth-seeking: the criminal trial. How can justice miscarry so egregiously, so unforgivably?

Ah, the word is broached: *forgive.*

It cannot be for any of us, participants in a way in the injustice done to these condemned innocents, to speak to them of forgiveness. But Jesus has already spoken powerfully, with his word and his example on the day of his execution: *"Father, forgive them, for they know not what they do."*

Rembert G. Weakland

The most difficult aspect of being a disciple of Christ is granting forgiveness. On the Cross Jesus gives us an example of that specifically Christian virtue. He even goes so far as to offer an excuse: they know not what they do.

St. Augustine [serm. 49.8] tells us that in his day some people omitted the section of the Our Father that said: Forgive us our sins as we forgive those who sin against us. In this phrase Augustine said they rightly recognized that they would be making a pact with God. By omitting it they felt they would not be bound in conscience. Such thinking must still have been common in the days of St. Benedict, since he prescribes [in chapter 13:12] that the superior in choir twice daily, that is, at Lauds and Vespers, say these words aloud for all to hear and thus renew their pact. Could this be the reason why in many of the oldest and best manuscripts of Luke's Gospels this verse, namely Jesus' words of forgiveness from the Cross, are so often omitted? Today no one omits these words. But perhaps the situation is worse in that we say them without taking into consideration their consequences.

Although we know this teaching of Jesus so well and have heard over and over again the many scriptural passages that reinforce it, we still are impressed in our day when someone acts accordingly. Instead, how frequently we hear people seeking vengeance rather than forgiveness. Perhaps we all suffer from a confusion of ideas. First, we know that justice must be done and confuse it with vengeance. Forgiveness is not to deny justice, but only to add the kind of mercy that we ourselves would want from others. Secondly, forgiveness does not mean to forget. Living with the memory of wrongs done can prevent us from their repetition. What forgiveness does is purify our own hearts and minds of hatred and vengeance and free us up. Thirdly, whether we sincerely ask for forgiveness or whether we seek to forgive others, ultimately we know what we really desire is reconciliation. Reconciliation goes beyond forgiveness in an attempt to expunge from our minds and from society all those obstacles that prevent all of us from living truly good, humane lives, concerned about the good of all.

What we need today are models and examples of true reconciliation. I think, for example, of the work of the reconciliation commission in South Africa led by Archbishop Tutu. Several photos of reconciliation in our day stay imbedded in our minds. I think of the embrace between Pope Paul VI and Patriarch Anthanagoras. I think also of the story of Cardinal Bernardin's forgiveness of his accuser and the reconciliation for the Eucharist that followed.

From the Cross Jesus is telling us that true reconciliation between peoples and among nations can only come when, like him, we are willing to forgive. He expects us then to say the Our Father as our daily prayer and as a renewal of our pact with him to forgive others as he forgives us.

MARY GONZALES

These words are perhaps the most profound revelation of God's love for us. This is the moment—suffering, betrayed, spat upon and reviled, made a laughing stock, nails driven through flesh, bones and tendons, a failure to friends, family, and foes—that Jesus utters this utterly unimaginable statement.

These are not just the words of a person scourged and humiliated. They are the words of a loving father protecting an immature son from a righteous judge. They are the words of a strong mother protecting a small child from a stern and stubborn father. These are words of unquestioning and unqualified love for others.

How can Jesus love his tormentors in this manner? He looks past their rage, past their foolishness and folly, past their cruelty, brutality, and depravity, past all their ugliness, and sees *human* beings worthy of love.

What a rebuke to those of us who cannot see humanity past a person's color, past a person's ethnic origin, past a person's gender, past a person's lifestyle, past a person's disability. How far we are as parents, as spouses, as citizens, as a nation, from Jesus' example of unquestioning and unqualified love. Father, forgive *us*.

DALLIN H. OAKS

Such were the first words from the Cross. To the rulers and people who mocked and taunted him, Jesus had maintained a kingly silence. But for the soldiers who drove the cruel nails into his hands and feet and hoisted him into the excruciating position that would drain away life in the most prolonged and painful way, Jesus prayerfully pleaded, *"Father, forgive them, for they know not what they do."*

The prophet Isaiah had foretold that the Messiah would be wounded for our transgressions and bruised for our iniquities, and with his stripes we would be healed (Isaiah 53:5). In Jesus' pleading for mercy for those whose enormous deed was done in ignorance, we see the fulfillment of Isaiah's messianic prophecy—"he hath poured out his soul unto death; and he was numbered with the transgressors; and he bare the sin of many, and made intercession for the transgressors" (Isaiah 53:12).

ADDIE L. WYATT

Here is this amazingly magnanimous Jesus! He hangs there on the Cross between two thieves. Notice, he doesn't curse or swear at those who were responsible for putting him there, as some of *us* might have done. He simply prays: *"Father, forgive them, for they know not what they do."*

This is true agape love, demonstrated at its best. A love that does not focus on self or circumstances. A love that does not hold grudges or seek revenge, but rather redeems.

No wonder the hymn writer could pen the words:

> Ere since by Faith
> I saw the stream
> Thy flowing wounds supply . . .
> Redeeming Love has been my theme,
> And shall be until I die!

> "There Is a Fountain" by William Cowper

How about you? Does Jesus Christ's example truly make the difference in the way you treat those who hurt, ridicule, or abuse you? Does his example truly make the difference in the way you face life, and the way you must ultimately face death?

If Easter is to have any real meaning for you, then why not experience the power of Christ's forgiving love as you too pray the prayer for your enemies: *"Father, forgive them, for they know not what they do."*

WILLIE CUSIC

In April 1999 the lives of two South Side Chicago mothers were forever changed. Their children—Eric and Shamika, both seventeen years of age—were enjoying each other's company on the front steps of her house. All of a sudden their laughter was transformed into horror as shots rang out. Shots that ended the life of a young man who was an honor student and an athlete. Shots that ended the life of a vibrant young woman who had just abandoned life in a gang and was looking forward to a promising future. Eric tried to protect Shamika from the gunfire by using his own body as a shield. But neither child had a chance.

Their deaths left their mothers grief-stricken and embittered. Their pain was so deep that the mere sight of each other brought back the bitterness of that tragic night. Just as the Good Friday story doesn't end with Jesus' crucifixion, the final chapter of this story is still being written. Both mothers will tell you that the healing process has been a difficult journey—a journey that first led them down the path of being crippled by pain, mired in malice, and consumed by hate. They were slowly sinking in the quicksand of revenge.

But their spirits were uplifted by Jesus' first words from the Cross: "Father, forgive them, for they know not what they do." They were challenged and comforted by the idea that Jesus could somehow forgive the very people who were murdering him! These mothers grappled with how to forgive themselves, then each other, and finally that faceless monster who killed their children. They are now standing at the threshold of unconditional forgiveness. The remainder of their journey will not be easy. But it's one they must endure in order to finally free themselves from the shackles of hatred and hopelessness.

As these two brave mothers complete the last mile of that journey, let us not be afraid to follow similar paths. For when we embrace the awesome power of forgiveness, we cheerfully trade all prior investments in vengeance and aggression for an overwhelming peace.

JEAN BETHKE ELSHTAIN

From the depths of his pain and torment, Jesus implores the heavenly father: please forgive them, spare my executioners from the burden of guilt they now bear, though they bear it unawares for they know not what they do.

We are overwhelmed by the pathos of this moment. It sears our minds and jolts our senses. It challenges our understanding of responsibility, guilt, and punishment. It invites the radical possibility of release from the crushing weight of our sins, our cruelties, the many ways that we throughout our lives torment others.

With a thoughtless word—she knows not what she does; with a reprimand shouted in rage that sends a frightened child fleeing in tears—he knows not what he does; with a cruel riposte, clever but cutting—she knows not what she does; with a face turned away in scorn or anger—he knows not what he does.

No more than our Lord's tormenters are we in full control of what we are doing at such moments. They were carrying out their orders. We are rushed and tired, or have run out of patience, or can't resist the opportunity to be clever or to be cruel.

Every day we nail Jesus to the Cross. Every day we must throw ourselves upon that cross, knowing that we will hear echoes of the words that have haunted all the bloody centuries since that terrible moment at Calvary, that crucifixion that uprooted our need for vengeance and would yet free us from our pettiness, our violence, and our deceit. Like the crucifiers so long ago, we may not know what we are doing at any given moment. But this we surely know: Lord, we are thine; crucified savior, pray for us. Father, forgive us for we know not what we do.

SEIICHI MICHAEL YASUTAKE

Here is genuine forgiveness. Peter asks Jesus, "how many times should I forgive my brother? 'til seven times?" Jesus answered, "Not seven times, but seventy times seven." *That* suggests unlimited, unconditional forgiveness.

Unconditional forgiveness is not just for individuals, but for groups of people—such as nations and federal authorities acting on their behalf. Jesus was convicted as a criminal by the Roman Empire and by the religious institution of his day. So, Jesus' unconditional forgiveness extended to his persecutors: the Roman Empire, the religious institution, and the common people who shouted "crucify him, crucify him!"

On Christmas or Easter, the theme is peace on earth—peace that does not yet exist. When our nation makes war on other nations, does our government know what it is doing?—or for that matter, do we the people know? When some demented soul murders a dozen people, that is horrible enough. But wars involve massive killings and desecration of God-given resources.

God realizes that we do not always know what we are doing. But God does know what God is doing. Only God's forgiveness of "seventy times seven" can break the chain of vengeance and violence continuing among nations.

God forgives us. Likewise we forgive others, no matter how unforgivable they seem. Thus Jesus empowers *us* through forgiveness to make way for justice and peace on earth.

MARTIN E. MARTY

Many ancient biblical manuscripts omit this cry. Scholars believe that Christian copyists in the second century could not stomach the idea that Jesus would want God to forgive his executioners. The scribes in that case did not have the generous soul that their Jesus here revealed, so they cut the saying out of their copies. Countless believers have done so ever since, whenever they failed to follow the one they call "savior"—whenever they've found someone not to forgive.

The cry for forgiveness is still a shocker, for those who have faith in Jesus, or for those who don't but like to have him as a model for their life. We all find it hard to imagine how liberating it can be when we stop finding a need to assign guilt, when we no longer need to hold a grudge, when we no longer seek revenge. No one finds it easy to ask forgiveness for someone else, because that means that we have to be forgivers ourselves.

So the scribes who took this text out of their manuscript were changing the whole plot of the Jesus story. They were simply taking out its heart.

DICK STAUB

Jesus lived in the same kind of world we do. Many people he met concluded, as we sometimes do, that some things are so bad that they simply cannot be forgiven.

In his public ministry Jesus taught these people they must forgive. He told the parable of the prodigal son—the story of a son who behaved absolutely unforgivably. Yet his father forgave him absolutely.

Now, suffering on the Cross, Jesus calls on the Heavenly Father to show forgiveness—even to those who are committing this seemingly unforgivable act.

There is comfort in knowing that God's forgiveness can be extended to us even when we are at our absolute worse. God understands we are like sheep that go astray. God knows that we often don't know what we are doing!

But there is also a challenge in Jesus' forgiving words. He once said, "If you forgive others, your Heavenly Father will forgive you. But if you do not forgive others, neither will your Father forgive your trespasses."

The early church understood this. Stephen when he was martyred cried out: "Lord lay not this sin to their charge." The apostle Paul reminded believers to forgive one another—even as God, for Christ's sake, has forgiven you.

We who take comfort in Jesus' words of forgiveness must also accept the challenge. No matter how we have been wronged, no matter how deep our pain, no matter how unjust the act against us, we must forgive—even as God, for Jesus' sake, has forgiven us.

William B. Spofford

It is a throne of pain:
      We know it as THE CROSS . . .
The first prayer from that height,
      a symbol of degradation,
      was for Others.
      Out of the betrayals—
          Out of the whippings—
               Out of the humiliations and
                   from nakedness—
      Out of the painful Wilderness of Aloneness—
      Comes, oh comes, a prayer for others!
      There THEY were . . . as there WE are . . .
      SKULL HILL is a high point in a throbbing city,
          a passionate place
          a powerful place and a place of pathos.
As they stood and as we stand beneath THE
          CROSS, we are CONVICTED.
          On that hill, beneath the CROSS, the ground is level:

"FATHER, FORGIVE THEM,
THEY DON'T KNOW WHAT THEY ARE DOING!"

      From the Cross-Throne, He could see all
the kingdoms of the world.
      And, so, the Last Temptation came:
      "LET THEM GO, GOD . . .
          THEY AIN'T WORTH IT!"
          But no,
             no,
                  no . . . instead,
      "FATHER, FORGIVE THEM!"

Then one of the criminals who were hanged blasphemed Him saying, "If you are the Christ, save yourself and us." But the other, answering, rebuked him, saying, "Do you not even fear God, seeing you are under the same condemnation? And we indeed justly, for we receive the due reward of our deeds; but this man has done nothing wrong." Then he said to Jesus, "Lord, remember me when you come into your kingdom." And Jesus said to him,

"SURELY, I SAY TO YOU, TODAY YOU WILL BE WITH ME IN PARADISE."

LUKE 23:39–43

BILLY GRAHAM

These two thieves were there, and they were laughing and jeering, but one of them suddenly stops. A strange look comes on his face. He looks at Jesus. He sees him dying, as lord of lords and king of kings. And there's something about his previous life that comes back to his thought. And he rebukes the other thief and he says, "Don't you fear God? This man hasn't done anything. He doesn't deserve to die. But you and I deserve to die. We deserve to be executed for our crimes." And he turns to Jesus and says, "Lord, remember me."

Look at his faith. If he had had this kind of faith at the tomb of Lazarus where he saw Jesus raise somebody from the dead, or when Jesus had walked on the water, or maybe at the Resurrection and stood at the open tomb—if he'd said, "Lord, remember me when you come into your kingdom." But to see Jesus on the Cross, dying and covered with blood, his hair matted with blood, and to see him dying in *that* condition, to have faith that this one in the center Cross was coming into a kingdom, and asking him to remember him—that took one of the greatest acts of faith in all the Bible.

And what was Christ's answer? What an answer he gave! The Bible says he'd been silent for quite a long time. But now he heard the cry of the thief, and he said, *"Today thou shalt be with me in paradise!"*

Well I want to tell you, if Jesus Christ would answer the prayer of that thief at that moment, he'll answer *your* prayer tonight.

PETER J. GOMES

I am notorious for getting lost while driving, and for not asking for directions—a man thing, I have been told. I may be lost, but I always know where I am. It is where I am going that is the problem.

The thief on the cross knew where he was. He was on the cross, hanging there as the just reward of his deeds. He did not offer alibi or apology. He did not explain himself a victim of circumstances. He was what he was, he knew what he was, and he knew where he was. He was, you might say, past all illusions. His co-conspirator understood that, and with an irreverence that shocks even now, he mocked Jesus with the cry we all know and use: "If you're so smart, how come you're up here with us?"

These crucified felons are not uninformed. They know who Jesus is supposed to be. They had heard of his mighty wonder working. Perhaps they had even heard of his raising Lazarus from the dead. Compared to that, getting them all down from the cross would be a piece of cake: *"If thou art the Christ, save thyself, and us, then."* Don't just stand there. Do something!

They know where *they* are, but that "good thief" is like you and like me. He's lost, not because he doesn't know where he is. He's lost because he doesn't know where he is going. So, very much unlike me, at least, he stops and asks for directions: *"Lord, remember me when you come into your kingly power."*

This is an act of faith: he places himself in the care of one who would appear to be no better off than he, and asks to be delivered to a place of kingly power the very thought of which is mocked by the reality of the Cross itself. He can see beyond that, he has what we call insight, a light that transcends what one can literally see. He moves not by sight, but by faith.

It seems too good to be true, too uncomplicated. But at death's door, things get pretty simple, pretty clear, pretty uncomplicated. The words belong to Jesus, but the future belongs to the thief: and for that we praise God.

Tim Costello

Jesus wasn't crucified between two candlesticks in a cathedral in a sacred place. He was crucified on the rubbish dump outside the city wall. He was crucified in a cosmopolitan, multicultural place where the inscription above him had to be written in Greek, in Hebrew, and in Latin. He was crucified in a place where soldiers gambled, where smut was talked, and where criminals shrieked in agony as they died.

There as one such criminal turned to him, understanding that his life of violence had now brought upon him his own punishment, his own death, Jesus spoke a word of truth, a word of reconciliation: *"Today you will be with me in paradise."*

The promise that whatever we have done in our lives, however we have lived, wherever we've slept, however we've treated people, God's grace is stronger, God's *"yes"* to us is more intense, God's forgiveness and love can embrace us. Here in this place of utter abandonment, a place of criminals and the horror and stench of death, was the promise that is life eternal for each of us: *"Today you will be with me in paradise."*

DEMETRI C. KANTZAVELOS

Orthodox Christians experience the living presence of Christ Jesus in the liturgical life of the Church. The liturgical tradition of the Greek Orthodox Church is simultaneously personal and communal, its dialectic reflected in the dialogue between our Crucified Lord and the repentant thief. This singular point, at the apex of the Lord's Passion, is at the center of what Orthodox Christians might call our mystical theology and spirituality.

At the solemn observance of the Crucifixion in the Orthodox tradition, a beautiful hymn frames the midpoint of our shared journey with our Savior. It is preceded by the thief's confession:

> Because of a tree, Adam was evicted from Paradise; because of the Tree of the Cross, the thief inhabited Paradise; for the former, in tasting, disobeyed the commandment of the Creator; the latter, crucified with You, confessed the concealed God. Savior, also remember us in Your Kingdom.

In the Orthodox mind and heart, both Adam and the thief are identified as recapitulating the whole of humanity. The sinful condition that is the result of our individual and collective "fallen-ness" seeks to possess what is not its own by nature. Adam in us all seeks to share in the God-Man's two natures, to be immortal. But our sinful nature propels us toward death, and the "wages of sin is death" (Romans 6:23). The only way to the Kingdom is through the death of the One who is both truly human and truly God: through Him, by Him and with Him. *"I say to you today, this day you will be with me in paradise."* This is the answer for all those who come to Christ Jesus in faith, humility, and hope.

The words provide not only hope for a future expectation, but the possibility of a present reality. Thus the word "today" is central to Christ's statement. Through the use of this word in prayer, the Orthodox consciousness awakens to a new awareness: a transcendent understanding of the temporal order. The Christ event is not simply recalled as a historical memory. It is lived mystically, in our present "now." Even the future is invoked as our present reality, in the living presence of Jesus Christ, who through the Holy Spirit is the same, "yesterday, today, and forever" (Hebrews 13:8).

For this reason, the Orthodox sing, *You abolished death by Your Cross; You opened Paradise to the thief . . ."* Opened to one thief, today opened to our human existence, the mystical communion between God and Humankind is made forever present and accessible at the foot of the Cross.

ALISON BODEN

Today.

This very day millions of hearts were shattered. It happened to people who heard words like, "It's malignant." "I don't love you anymore." "There's been an accident." Today, around the world, millions of lives were forever changed. It happened to people who heard words like, "She's healthy and beautiful, ten fingers and ten toes." "The tests came back clean as a whistle." "Marry me." Today—and every day—the universe is unalterably turned on its head for untold numbers of God's children.

"Today," Jesus said to the thief nailed up next to him. Today. We know about this thief only two things—first, he was guilty of thievery, and second, that he believed that Jesus would be ruler of a realm completely unlike the one that had nailed both of them up to die—to suffocate, actually—in agony. The thief states that plainly: "Jesus, remember me when you come into your kingdom."

What a moment. Conversation between two men in the very process of dying. Nails through their hands and feet, the weight of their suspended bodies on the sinews of their insteps and palms, and they talk! They talk about today. They talk about the flipping of their universe—today. They talk about seeing one another in Paradise before the sun on which they gaze goes down. As the life drips out of them, they talk. And neither of them will have to die alone.

That would be the way of Jesus who throughout his life welcomed the lowest to be by his side. Jesus would enter Paradise leading not a saint or a beloved friend, but a common criminal! Like that thief still on the cross, some of us this evening know that we are dying. The rest of us don't want to think about the fact that we are dying, although we have been since we first drew breath. The tragedy isn't that all of us are dying; that's just a fact of being human. The tragedy is that some of us aren't living, like that thief begins living in his last hour of life. That's when he meets Jesus and realizes that Christ will soon reign over a realm that he could never have dreamed of, and he asks to have a place there with him. Christians believe that all are offered citizenship with Jesus, that all may come to life, as did that thief as he died—as we die. Today.

B. Herbert Martin Sr.

The Gospel of Luke contains one of the most dramatic stories in the whole Bible: when on the Cross of Calvary, the Lord was crucified. The mob stood around him and mocked him, and two thieves were nailed beside him to share the agony. But one of them cried out to him, "Oh Lord, remember me."

As this thief was about to die, he turned to Jesus for resolutions Christ accepted him, saying: *"Today you will be with me in paradise."*

The dying criminal had more faith than the rest of Jesus' followers put together. Although the disciples continued to love Jesus, their hopes for the kingdom were shattered. Most of them had gone into hiding. By contrast, the thief looked at the man who was dying next to him and said, "Jesus, remember me when you come into your kingdom." By all external appearances, the kingdom was finished. But how inspiring to us is the faith of this dying criminal who saw beyond the present shame, defeat, darkness, tragedy, and violence to the coming power and glory of God's kingdom.

The thief was saved by grace. It was a gift of God. He did not deserve it and he could not earn it. We too have this grace available to us. In spite of our hurts, our pain, and our historical woundedness, His grace is still sufficient for us. Won't you accept God's mercy and grace—that you too will see beyond your present darkness, tragedy, and shame, to the power and glory of a transformed life in Christ by crying out Lord, remember me!

LANDIS H. MCALPIN

The word "paradise" has evoked many thoughts and responses down through the years. The term suggests that which is most desirable, a place of peace, a place where everyone is happy—certainly a place where there is no hard labor. It is all of this, but more. Christians believe it is the place where Christ is—a descriptive name for heaven.

The second word of Jesus personalizes our relationship with God. We will not be just like a visitor walking through the park. Talking to a common thief, Jesus informs us, you will be with me. These words echo down the corridors of time to generations yet unborn. The scripture tells us that this thief had transgressed the laws of God and man, and deserved to be punished. He'd once been a member of a synagogue, but had become an enemy of society. The Judicatories had decreed that he was beyond redemption, and that his crime was punishable by death. So he and another thief were crucified that day, alongside Jesus.

Hanging from his cross, that thief came to believe at the last possible moment that Jesus was the Christ—that he who believes shall be saved, saved by grace. It was here that the thief made his last-minute conversion, saying to Jesus, "Lord, remember me when thou comest into thy kingdom." Hanging from his own cross, Jesus answered, "Verily I say unto you, this day shalt thou be with me in paradise."

It's not too late for us to be remembered, through the amazing grace of Jesus.

YVONNE D. HAWKINS

When we hear the story about the two dying thieves, I find it interesting that Luke left out so many personal details. Without them, we really don't know what made one thief say, "If you really are the king, for real, why don't you just save yourself—and while you're at it, save me too!" We can only guess why the second thief told the first, "Man, just shut up! You don't know what you're talkin' about. This guy, *he* didn't do nothin' wrong, but you and me, we're gettin' what we deserve." We don't know what then motivated him to say, "Jesus, when you come into your kingdom, remember me."

Oh the questions we could ask! Questions like what psycho-social factors were going on here? What were their families like? Was there abuse going on in their homes? And by the way, what were their specific crimes? We assume these guys weren't everyday purse-snatchers from the streets of Jerusalem.

It's interesting that all of this information was simply left out. But the omission speaks volumes. It says *it doesn't matter*. It doesn't matter who your mama was. It doesn't matter who your daddy was. It doesn't matter how many brothers or sisters you had. It doesn't even matter if you grew up on the wrong side of the tracks. None of that matters. When the nitty hit the gritty, the *only* thing that mattered was that each thief had an opportunity. And to the one who took it, Jesus said, "*Today you will be with me in paradise.*"

When I was a child growing up, I remember hearing preachers say over and over that you could come to Jesus just as you are. You could be a gambler, but just come. You could be a prostitute, just come. You could be an addict, but just come. And Jesus would accept you. But I was always curious why they talked about people like *that* because I didn't know anyone like that. I knew people like *me*. And I'd wonder, what about people like me, people who mean so well but who still mess up so bad? Could *we* come too?

I'm here to tell you that it doesn't matter who you are or where you come from. All that matters is what you believe—whether you believe that Jesus can rescue us, even from ourselves. And as long as we have just one last, dying breath, that's enough. That's all we need. Because the *only* thing that matters is whether or not we believe. For those who do, Jesus promises, *"Today, THIS day, you WILL be with me in paradise!"*

ROBERT LUDWIG

We are told by the Gospel according to Luke that Jesus was executed with two others, identified as "criminals." They were likely bandits—peasant resisters who had been forced off their land and had taken to the hills. Such people were regarded by the authorities as criminals, but considered by the peasant people themselves "as heroes, as champions, avengers, fighters for justice . . . leaders of liberation . . . men to be admired, helped, and supported"—Eric Hobsbawn, *Bandits,* 2nd ed. (Middlesex: Penguin Books, 1985), p. 17.

Jesus and they, peasant resisters all, faced execution by crucifixion—a horrible, tortuous, and public event meant to intimidate by instilling fear into the hearts of Jewish peasants. They would become examples to anyone who would challenge Caesar's rule in Galilee.

Luke tells us that one of these execution victims turned to Jesus and said, *"Remember me when you come into your kingdom."* To which Jesus responded, *"I tell you this: today you shall be with me in paradise."*

Jesus' revolution was grounded in spirit—in a radical trust in God, who loves the poor. The lowly and the marginal, those at the edge of society, then and now, hear the Gospel and give themselves over to God. We dare not be intimidated by this Cross. Rather, let us join our voices to that of this rebel bandit—to all those in our world who are homeless and have nothing: "Jesus, remember us; inspire us; help us give ourselves in trust, not to our rule or that of Caesar, but to the rule of God."

LEROY A. MITCHELL

Luke, the physician, is the only Gospel writer to include the two thieves at the Crucifixion with Jesus. Nevertheless, the presence of thieves fits into the ministry that Christ established during his three years of preaching and teaching. He could be found with those for whom others had no hope. And the thieves' response to Jesus in this situation was no surprise to him; it was similar to what had happened throughout his ministry. There were those who doubted his message as well as those who believed it. However there was one thief who was willing to be honest and truthful at his hour of death. This criminal knew he deserved to die for his wrong, but Jesus who had done nothing wrong did not deserve the same punishment. Even though he was nailed to a cross, this thief sought one word of hope at the end of his life from a man, a savior, who was experiencing the same pain and humiliation. Jesus responded to the thief's request to be remembered with good news: *"I tell you the truth, today you will be with me in paradise."*

Hope was not only kept alive that afternoon for one thief on a cross in the Place of the Skull, but that same hope has been extended to us this day when hope seems so allusive.

GROVER A. ZINN

The drama of Christ's seven last words moves our focus from person to person, group to group, emotion to emotion. Now the two thieves who were crucified with Jesus come to the center of our vision. One thief mocks Jesus, who hangs, despised and rejected, upon the Cross; the other thief sees in the midst of suffering and death a truth revealed, a truth from God. That thief cries out for deliverance: *"Lord, remember me when you come into your kingdom."* In the midst of a pain-wracked death by crucifixion, Christ gives the greatest gift he can—not a miraculous transformation but a new hope in the midst of death: *"This day you shall be with me in paradise."* Jesus doesn't ask the thief who he is, what he has, or what he has done. He hears the thief's plea and responds with a gift.

In a world of suffering, death, and destruction, Christ does not offer life bathed in sentimental goodness. He asks us to enter pain and feel sorrow. Just as sorrow and love were mingled in his blood and sweat, so in *our* lives love is known in the midst of pain, and deliverance can come in times of deepest darkness. The mystery of the crucifixion, indeed the mystery of the thief, is the mystery of love—love hidden and revealed in the bloody death of Christ, hanging on a wooden cross on a lonely hill outside Jerusalem.

When Jesus saw his mother
and the disciple whom
he loved standing near,
he said to his mother,

"WOMAN, BEHOLD YOUR SON!"

Then he said to his disciple,

"BEHOLD YOUR MOTHER!"

And from that hour the disciple
took her to his own home.

John 19:26–27

KELLY CLEM

It is perhaps the most difficult thing a mother should ever have to face: watching her own child's death. Yet Mary stayed near her son. We can only imagine *her* thoughts and feelings. The helplessness of watching him suffer . . . the loneliness of touching his body for the last time . . . wishing that maybe *she* could be the one to hang in his place. . . . And don't you know, that she let out a defiant cry of *"No!"* that went unanswered.

Jesus must have known her feelings, for even as he suffered, he looked to his mother and to his beloved disciple, and he entrusted them to each other's care. Jesus was trying to teach them that "family" is so much more than those with whom we live. Family is made up of those who love you and care for your spirit. Even in his last moments of life, Jesus tried to tell those who loved him the most that they would not be left alone.

Camilla Burns

Mary appears twice in the Gospel of John—at Cana and at the Cross. In both appearances, she is associated with the disciples of Jesus. The story at Cana takes place in the context of the completion of the call of the disciples, while the Cana story ends with the recognition of belief as the culmination of discipleship—"and his disciples believed in him." At the foot of the Cross, John is the representative of all disciples.

At Cana and the Cross, Jesus refers to Mary as woman. Although the title may be difficult to contemporary ears, it identifies Mary as representative. Woman cannot be understood in terms of ordinary familial relations. Rather than a relationship of kinship, something new is being birthed. Mary is now the mother of all disciples. John, the representative of all disciples, and the mother of all disciples forge a new community.

The ministry of Jesus that began at a wedding in a Galilean village is completed by the formation of a new relationship between a woman and a man at the Cross. Two people connected by their common faith relationship with Jesus rather than kinship ties form the nucleus of a new community. In their relationship with each other they represent the community of believers.

Mary's intervention at Cana is rejected on the grounds that Jesus' hour had not yet come, but at the Cross we are in the context of Jesus' hour—his passion, death, and resurrection. Mary was denied a role at Cana when she intervened simply as Jesus' physical mother; she is most truly his mother in this "hour" of God's plan when she brings forth the Christian community in the image of her son. The suffering at the foot of the Cross becomes the birth pangs of the new community.

As we stand at the foot of the Cross with Mary, we witness the birth of the Christian community. *"Behold your son!" "Behold your mother!"* are words of a new relationship binding today's believers in a Christian community. In their relationship with each other they represent the community of believers. Mary and John are the recipients of the love of Jesus that extends to those who believe in him. This moment begins the faith community that extends into the future and includes all "who have not seen, yet believe."

JEAN BETHKE ELSHTAIN

Behold! To hold, to look upon, to see, to regard. To see the face of another and to be obliged. Behold! Do not turn away. Hold! Do not be afraid. Jesus here calls us to a moment of recognition. Behold, thy son. See him with your own eyes. Behold, thy mother. Look into her face. Take her into your heart, your home. And this under the most terrible of circumstances. The torment and death of one who was son, who was friend, who was teacher. But who now takes leave of us until we regard one another again in the kingdom to come.

89

Jesus, taking leave of mother, of disciple, looking down from the Cross and in the very moment of His passion, charges those He loves to love one another. Abandoned, He refuses to abandon. Tormented, He refuses to torment. Suffering, He calls us to succor. Dying, He calls us to life. Do not lock your hearts. Do not close your eyes. Behold: she is before you. Behold: he stands along side you. Mother and son. Father and daughter. Brother and sister. Master and disciple. Love one another even as I have loved you. For Jesus knows: the Father calls us to a wider fellowship. We first behold those who share our homes. But all the parents and children who are forlorn are here recalled and we are called to see them, to hear them, for the Lord's sake.

RITA SIMÓ

With these words Jesus showed us his love in a very human way. He understood the sadness his mother and friend were experiencing, and he wanted to let them know that he was not abandoning them.

But there is another message. Jesus is reminding us of our obligation to be responsible and supportive, to be companions to each other—not just to our friends and family, but to everyone with whom we come in contact, regardless of their color, shape, age, nationality, religion, and even those with whom our country is at war.

The Gospel continues: *"from that hour the disciple took her to his own home."* Several years ago I knew a family with two kids. The mother and father were seized and deported by immigration officials after a raid at the factory where they worked. Their biggest fear was what would happen to their kids. How would they be taken care of until things could be worked out? Without a second thought, a generous family from across the hall in their apartment building agreed to take the kids and provide for them until they could be reunited with their parents. That's what this is about!

How will *we* respond when we encounter situations dealing with homelessness, sexual or physical abuse, or other injustices? Let us hope that we use the grace given to us to respond as real companions, to provide the unconditional support that Jesus asks of us—not just when it's convenient, but at every possible opportunity.

JAMES MURRAY

In his suffering, Christ forgets himself, and in an ultimate intimacy, heals his broken family by asking his mother to embrace John as a son, and John to look upon Mary as his mother. There is pathos in this commitment. Nailed, fighting for breath, unable even to reach out to his own mother or to touch his most beloved friend, yet Jesus reaches out. He speaks, *"Woman, behold your son." "Son, behold your mother."*

Amid the ignominy of the Cross, Jesus creates a home. He gives them dignity and pride. He makes a cosmic leap. The world becomes a family united by suffering. But it is more than that. God is dismayed by human cruelty and wishes to assuage it by love. In the dark womb of Calvary, on a hill like a skull, a new way of loving is born. The scandal being perpetrated, the execution of a perfectly good man, might well have justified God's turning vindictive and wiping out the entire human race. Instead he transformed it into a family—mothers and sons, fathers and daughters its impulse. Behold the miracle of the love of God.

ELIZABETH-ANNE STEWART

Battered, bruised, torn and blistered,
bloodied by vicious thorns, the sting of the whip,
and by the terrible weight of wood,
our Saviour was finally "straightened out,"
stripped of comfort,
un-bent of any illusions
upon the rack of the scandalous cross.
Looking down, arms outstretched,
contorted like a question mark
between heaven and earth,
he beheld his mother and his beloved disciple:
"Woman," he said, *"this is your son."*
Then to the disciple he said, *"This is your mother."*
And his mother, beholding him,
the one she had cradled,
felt the thrust of Simeon's sword
pierce her womb
like bitter labor pangs
and, as her time drew near—
the time of death, not birth—
the disciple clung to her,
his mother, the mother of sorrows,
the mother of us all . . .

GREGORY DELL

The eighteen-year-old young man already had attempted suicide twice. The torment and isolation were simply too great. Now, away from home for the first time, he wrote the careful letter to his parents.

> Dear Mom and Dad,
> There is no easy way to say this. I am gay—what you call "homosexual."
> I need your help and love. Who else could understand me?

He waited. Five days later the envelope came. With fear on the edge of terror, and hope that he dared not admit, he opened the paper and found its only contents: his birth certificate torn in pieces.

The word of Christ at the moment of his greatest agony was a radical word of love and grace. His message: You belong to a family which not even death can destroy. Earthly fear or ignorance, weakness or bigotry or even violence may tear into pieces the world's affirmation of your value and goodness. But I say to you, there is a God who surrounds you with the true love of a mother and the faithfulness of a true child. That love and faithfulness may not be where you had hoped or yearned. But it is there. I give it to you—without conditions. *"Woman, behold your son." "Son or daughter, behold your mother."*

Rachel Thompson

Jesus knows that death is near, that his long suffering is almost at an end. He looks down and through his agony sees his mother standing near the foot of the Cross.

His mother. There is the woman who has loved him, in the way of mothers, his whole life long. Who fled with him to Egypt to save his infant life. Who searched frantically for him when he was lost as a child. Who tried to restrain him from preaching and healing when she feared for his sanity and wanted to protect him. Who, hoping to see him, was kept waiting outside with the crowds while he sat inside with his disciples, pondering the deepest meanings of kinship. Perhaps she never really understood his work. Perhaps, in the way of mothers, what she cared about most, what she prayed for, was his safety. And now she stands with the other women, watching as her child dies an unendurable death. Imagine.

Most of the men abandoned Jesus when he was arrested, but there is one who did not. Standing with Mary near the Cross is the Beloved Disciple. And Jesus, looking down, loving this steadfast woman, wishes to give what he could never receive—safety and protection. *"Woman, here is your son,"* he says gently to her. And to his friend, *"Here is your mother"*— thus giving them to one another. And with these words, this mother and this dying son, filled with love for each other, filled with sorrow, complete their earthly circle.

MICHAEL L. PFLEGER

From the Cross at Calvary, Jesus completed his last will and testament. He had already committed his blood to the church, his garments to his enemies, forgiveness to a crucifying crowd, a thief to paradise, and would soon commend his spirit to his father and his body to the grave.

But here in this third word from the Cross, Jesus takes time out from dying to commend you and I to each other. To give us to each other. To remind us that he came not only to reconcile, restore, and reconnect you and I to his father, but to reconcile, restore, and reconnect you and I to each other. We cannot say we love God whom we do *not* see, and not love our brothers and sisters whom we *do* see.

From Calvary's Cross Jesus looks beyond the pain of his body to address the pain of his body. Jesus recognizes that not only does it take a whole village to raise a child, but what is really needed is a new village. For the present village is sick, divided, disconnected, and dismembered. The body of Christ is still being pierced and crucified. We have built a society and a Christianity that have made the addicted feel like our burden; the AIDS patient feel like a plague; the prostitute society's throw-away; our elders forgotten and useless; and where racism still continues to be America's greatest addiction, not only in the work house and market house, but also in the church house.

Jesus took time out from dying to reconcile, restore, and reconnect us to each other, to make us accountable for each other, so that we would not become the modern day Pilates, seeking to wash our hands from each other's responsibility. The truth is, you and I are not our brothers' keepers. You and I *are* our brother and our sister. And the village is in our hands.

"Woman, behold your son." "Son, behold your mother."

JOHN M. BUCHANAN

June 22, 1944, is a day I will never forget. I was six years old. A telegram arrived that day informing my grandmother and my mother that my Uncle Jack—Private First Class, John Calvin McCormick, USMC, twenty-four years old—had been killed in action in the Pacific on the island of Saipan.

He was my mother's baby brother—my grandmother's youngest of a family of eight, a late-comer, ten years between him and my mother. He was the red-haired delight of their life. Now he was dead, and never had I seen such grief. I have not witnessed grief like it since.

Young men should not die. Parents should not experience the death of their children. Everything about that is wrong, out of sync. Children are supposed to bury their parents, not the other way around.

And so a small, poignant, tragic, personal moment happens in the midst of events that will loom large in human history—the crucifixion of God's son, the death, for the salvation of humankind, of Jesus the Christ. And in the midst of its terrible beauty a touchingly personal event: a son watching his mother *watch him* die. Reaching out, as best he could to her in love—to assure her protection and security. Reaching out to his dearest friend, who perhaps was alone in the world, extending to him the nurture and steady love which his mother had given *him* every day of his life.

In the midst of the story of God's love and the salvation of humankind, there is a personal encounter: a mother and her son, a son and the friend he loved—a small personal anecdote to remind us that his love is intimate and personal. It embraces us as we, too, watch as he dies.

From noon on, darkness
came over the whole land
until three in the afternoon.
And about three o'clock,
Jesus cried with a loud voice,

"ELI, ELI, LAMA
SABACHTHANI?—
MY GOD, MY GOD,
WHY HAVE YOU
FORSAKEN ME?"

MATTHEW 27:45–46

MARTIN E. MARTY

That is a cry of abandonment! Many believers since have tried to explain it away, saying that Jesus was only quoting Psalm 22, which ends on a note of confidence. No, that doesn't work. This quoted cry became his own statement of his *own* condition, in that eerie darkness of that afternoon. He may have been ready for an innocent death, he was sure of his purpose, but in that pain, and in that chaos, and in that hour, he had nothing left but a cry of God-forsakenness.

That cry, of course, belongs to the larger plot of the Gospel story, of faith in Jesus and the one he called Eli—my God. If he had *not* felt abandoned, his dying would have been only an uncomfortable charade on the way to a resurrection. Here instead is the note of realism that has led believers ever since to have confidence that he was the *last* one who needed to feel utterly abandoned by God. In their view, full of faith, thanks to the love he showed the world, he effected a new relation to God. And so they are confident that they will live and die in divine company—never forsaken as he felt he was, and at that moment, as he *truly was*.

Peter S. Knobel

In his own darkest hour Jesus invokes the powerful words of the Psalmist David to express the depth of his pain. The despairing words of the Psalm continue: "Why are you so far from helping me, from the words of my groaning? O my God, I cry by day, but you do not answer and by night, but find no rest." In our distress we cry out to God only to experience a terrifying silence. God who should be our refuge and our fortress does not even appear as a whisper of hope.

Perhaps the most poignant word in the verse is Lama: Why? It seems like a theological question but it is really an existential question. David and Jesus who were people of faith were not immune to the reality of human suffering. They, like so many other people, experienced the slings and arrows of human callousness and human evil. They, like so many others, knew the unpredictable tragedies of disease and natural disaster. They were people who were in relationship with God, but they understood that God is both presence and absence.

Does God withdraw from us? Or is it we who withdraw from God? Again the question seems theological but it is existential. Neither David nor Jesus is a reclusive mystic. They are engaged with the daily struggles of the use of power, injustice, disease, hunger, and poverty. Their *cri de coeur* is directed at the human condition in an unredeemed world. In their anguish, they know that the world is not yet healed from the limitations that creation imposes on God. Their words express the pain of God who is also crying, "My Children, My Children, Why have you forsaken Me?" It is the mutuality of divine and human suffering which creates a solidarity of pain.

The suffering God and suffering humanity are joined in the words of David and Jesus. The divine pathos means that God and humankind need each other. God is healed when human beings lift up the fallen, heal the sick, free the captive, clothe the naked, and feed the hungry. God is healed when a loving hand wipes the tear of a child. God is healed when we look into each other's eyes and see the face of God. When we forsake each other, we drive God's presence from the world. God is absent when we are absent. Every time we hear the words "Eli, Eli, Lama Sabachtani?—My God, My God, why have you forsaken me?" know that God is also saying: "My Children, My Children, Why have you forsaken Me?" Then we must embrace the pain of others and draw God down from heaven toward the earth so that darkness will give way to endless light.

VIRGIL P. ELIZONDO

What an incredible love Jesus showed for all of us! For there is no greater love than to share in the deepest agony of the beloved. Jesus, in his own body and spirit, shared our excruciating pains of embarrassment, shame, failure, alienation, loneliness, and distress. Because of this unlimited love for us, God raised him to eternal life.

When I feel totally down in the affairs of life, I need not fear, I need not despair. For I know that the son of God is with me, to give me that hope beyond all human hope, that God—no mere human—will triumph in me. In the abandonment of Jesus, I am rescued from my own abandonment. Abandonment never again! For God is with me no matter what.

Gary Miller

It is frightening to think of Jesus feeling abandoned by God. If the one who was so intimate with his Father could be so forsaken, it is not surprising that in times of loneliness, illness, economic stress, death or many of the other ills which we experience, we too feel that God is very distant from us—that He has abandoned us in our time of greatest need.

In a recent letter by Cardinal Joseph Bernardin, written especially to those experiencing illness but also very inspiring to all people, he shared these reflections:

> No matter how strong our faith may be, we are still human, and we cannot always control our feelings and emotions; indeed we should not. There is no contradiction between having deep faith in Jesus and his saving power and, at the same time, experiencing fear, anxiety, and frustration. Our faith gives us a perspective that enables us to deal positively and realistically with these realities and see beyond them. Our faith, indeed, is the basis for our hope.

The feeling of abandonment Jesus experienced on the Cross was real. The feelings *we* have of abandonment in *our* crises are real. But feelings are not faith. Our feelings are conditioned by the human experience of the moment. Faith is beyond the human experience; it draws us into the mystery of God and his love for us—a love that is permanent and unchanging, no matter what the human condition of the moment is.

Jesus' prayer was real; our prayer is real. The feelings are real; but so is God's promise of never abandoning those he loves. Jesus' death on the Cross brought him through the pain of feeling abandoned into the glory of Resurrection—a pledge and promise to us of the reality of faith overcoming the feelings which can obscure the vision of glory.

STEVEN SHOEMAKER

As Matthew and Mark tell the story of the death of Jesus, these were the very last words he spoke before "breathing his last" and "giving up the Spirit." Like all the words from the Cross, these are quotations from the Hebrew Scriptures, the Jewish Bible, the Tanakh, these from Psalm 22. These words— very human cries of agony, loneliness, fear, pain, and abandonment—were so shocking that they were not recorded by Luke or John, perhaps because both wanted to emphasize more the divinity of Christ.

Both Matthew and Mark recorded this saying in Aramaic as well as in Greek. Maybe Jesus was remembering the Psalms memorized in the Aramaic language of his childhood. Psalm 22 begins with these words, then in the Hebrew poetic form of parallelism, echoes them with "Why are you so far from helping me, from the words of my groaning?" The Gospel writers do not presume to tell us how Jesus felt immediately before death. They record no interior monologue. But they give us his words. In quoting from one of the most famous Jewish Psalms of lament, Jesus reaches deeply into the heart of his Jewish faith. He does not quote from the very next Psalm, the 23rd Psalm. He does not say "God is my shepherd; nothing do I lack . . ." No, his quotation is from one of the Psalmist's loud cries of woe.

The surprise is that Christians confess Jesus to be truly God even in this moment of being ever so truly human when he cries out: "My God, my God, why have you abandoned me?"

DANIEL ISAAK

This last painful cry of Jesus on the Cross, according to the book of Matthew and recorded also by Mark, comes directly from the opening of the 22nd Psalm. The Book of Psalms is attributed to David, who lived better than a thousand years before the events recorded in the Christian Scriptures. Some biblical commentators maintain that in this particular Psalm, David, either during the persecution of King Saul or when confronted by the aggressive Philestine forces, laments his own distress. In the Talmud it is even suggested that the words of the psalmist are a prophetic reference to the plight of the Jews during Haman's plot of annihilation, later recorded in the Book of Esther.

Perhaps a most apropo association, as we now contemplate these words, is to connect them to a show tune written for the Yiddish theater in 1896, over a hundred years ago. This tune became a devotional prayer, far outliving the play for which it was originally composed. In much the same way in which these words remind Christians of Jesus' pain and suffering, the song *"Eyli, Eyli,"* which begins with the words of the psalmist, *"My God, my God, why hast Thou forsaken me?"* likewise prompts thoughts in Jews of persecution and abandonment.

In Nazi-occupied Poland, the singer most closely associated with *"Eyli, Eyli"* was Miriam Eisenstadt, a beautiful young woman, still in her teens, whose radiant charm and extraordinary voice had won her an affectionate title, "the nightingale of the Warsaw Ghetto." Miriam Eisenstadt evoked so much feeling that when she sang this song, she moved even the stony hearts of ghetto officials and the police. Her fame was so widespread that when the Nazis sent a crew into the ghetto to make a "documentary" of the life of the Jews there, she was compelled to appear in the film and sing *"Eyli, Eyli."* In the final days, when the ghetto Jews were being rounded up and sent off to the camps, Miriam Eisenstadt refused to be separated from her parents as they were being herded into a cattle car. So an impatient guard shot and killed her. By the age of nineteen, "the nightingale of the Warsaw Ghetto" had sung her last song.

T. L. BARRETT

This is a powerful expression, made even more powerful because Jesus prefaced it with the exclamation: *"my God!"* He is saying, no matter what you put me through, no matter what you allow them to do to me, I am not letting go of you. You are still *my God.* Jesus was in the midst of agony, yet rather than chastising God, he embraces God.

There were nails in his hands—yet he cries, *"my God!"*

Spikes were driven through his feet—nevertheless, *"my God!"*

He wore a crown with seventy-two razor-sharp thorns, puncturing his blood vessels, causing excruciating pain—but you are still *"my God!"*

Worst of all, it felt like God had abandoned him. And indeed, God *did* abandon him so that none of *us* will ever be abandoned by God. But Jesus did not forsake God. Jesus never renounced his embrace, his love, his oneness with his God.

Vincent L. Wimbush

Of the "seven last words," these are the most haunting and riveting, the most disturbing and unfathomable. They are so because they are unexpected. What reader would expect the self-possessed, wisdom teacher figure of the Matthean story to express himself with such emotion? They are so because of the dramatic scene—a crucifixion, the most public and humiliating of ancient world punishments—in which they occur. They are so because they constitute a question (the only one among the "seven last words"—an awful, pathetic, wrenching question to which no answer is given, to which no answer is possible). They are so because of the question actually posed: following the evangelist Mark in taking the question directly from Psalm 22:1, the evangelist Matthew makes the question on the lips of Jesus a disturbing and unfathomable one for listeners and readers of every age.

The question cuts to the core of the puzzle about the meaning of human existence from a particular site of interpretation reflecting a particular set of experiences: What has *God* to do with this? *Where* is God in all of this? It is the challenge of a human-sensitive figure challenging all others—including God—to take account of unexplained, unjustified, unexpected perduring pain, suffering, forsakenness that defines human experience. Both the Psalm 22 reference and the larger narrative context in which the question is raised make it clear that God has everything and nothing to do with human suffering. God is responsible for all things (witness the darkness occurring at midday) and God is nowhere to be found. Yet Jesus, as the story goes, experiences victory. So Jesus' question jolts all readers into seeing that the attempt to fathom and address the puzzle of human hurt and forsakenness is the only means to human hopefulness and victory.

MARK A. NOLL

This is the only time in the New Testament that Jesus addresses God without calling him "Father." The words are taken from the beginning of the 22nd Psalm, a psalm that ends in triumph for the believer. But it is not triumph that fills the being of Jesus here. It is suffering, abandonment, anguish, dereliction. The one who was called "The Light of the World" now is wrapped in thick darkness.

According to traditional Christian theology, Jesus bears on the Cross the sin of the world. This cry gives voice to the separation from God that is the consequence of sin. It is dreadful beyond the telling. Yet at the end of a century like our own, where the cry of dereliction has been heard again and again, we do well to note that even at this most agonizing moment, Jesus calls upon God as "*my* God." And so, following him, may we.

Niles Elliot Goldstein

These are the last words of Jesus in Matthew and Mark as he confronts the end of his life. These are also the words of David, written down centuries before as he composed Psalm 22 in a state of loneliness and despair. Why would spiritual souls like these call out to their God with such a profound sense of abandonment, as if the figure they most loved in all the world, the great sovereign to whom they owed their very beings, had left them to die on a cross, or, as David says, to perish in "the mouth of a lion?"

Even for those of us who believe in God, constant faith is difficult to maintain. When bad things happen to good people, when injustice, like a moth, eats away at the fabric of our communities, we feel that God is far away, that God has abandoned us to an indifferent or hostile universe. But God has not. Though there are times when God seems as close as a whisper, there are other times when God must take a step back. In Jewish mysticism there is a concept called *tzimtzum*—"contraction." According to this idea, in order to create the world God needed first to withdraw from it—so that the earth and her creatures wouldn't drown in an ocean of divine omnipresence. What we view as God's distance can be, in truth, just the opposite. What seems to us like indifference can be, to God, an expression of love—a way of letting destiny unfold, of preserving human freedom, of giving us room to breathe.

And so, when we too cry out, *"My God, why have you forsaken me?"* we shouldn't be surprised if God answers, "because I love you with all my heart."

JEREMIAH A. WRIGHT JR.

The most human cry from the Cross was not that statement which articulated a biological need ("I thirst"). It was, rather, the critical question that pointed to a theological need. From Job through Jeremiah and from Samuel through the Psalmist, the question "Why" had been raised by people of faith.

Why? Why do the evil prosper? Why has cancer attacked my body? Why me? Why did God let my child die? Why did God take away from me the one person who made life meaningful for me? Why won't God answer me? Why has God forsaken me?

Jesus cried out in anguish from the Cross these same words: "My God! My God! Why hast thou forsaken me?" Some say he was quoting Psalm 22:1 as he felt the full weight of abandonment. He felt that he had been abandoned not only by those who fled in the Garden; not only by those who thronged the path leading into Jerusalem; not only by the many who followed him from Capernaum and Nain through Jericho, hanging on his every word and bringing their sick to be healed by him. He felt that he had been abandoned not only by Peter, James, and John. Most devastatingly, he felt that he had also been abandoned by God. And to be abandoned by God is the ultimate abandonment! The agony of his soul brought the words of Psalm 22 to his mind.

Many of us have felt what Jesus felt that day. Many of us still wrestle with that ultimate faith question. And to that question God responds through the Prophet Isaiah:

When you pass through the waters
I will be with you;
and through the rivers
they shall not overwhelm you.
When you walk through the fire
you shall not be burned,
nor shall the flame consume you
for I am the Lord your God . . .
Fear not
for I am with you!

We are not forsaken or forgotten! Immanuel means God is with us—even when we feel abandoned.

Knowing that all things were now accomplished, that the scripture might be fulfilled, Jesus said,

"I THIRST."

A jar of sour wine was standing there. So they put a sponge full of the wine on a branch of hyssop and held it to his mouth.

JOHN 19:28–29

DALLIN H. OAKS

All that Jesus said in his first four utterances from the Cross ministered to
the needs of others, or concerned his messianic mission. Even the agonies
of crucifixion could not wring out words of personal complaint or concern
from the one who had been chosen as the sacrificial lamb without blemish.
Until he had fulfilled his mission to be afflicted and suffer and shed his
blood as an atonement for the sins and sorrows of all, the Savior of the
world had no thought of himself. Only when his incomprehensibly painful
burden had been carried to its appointed conclusion, only when he had
accomplished his mission, did he yield to the physical pain. He did so with
only two words: *"I thirst."*

Martin E. Marty

Of course, no one heard Jesus shout, "I am hungry," because Jesus did not shout it, would not have shouted it. Hunger is secondary to thirst in human need. The Gospel writers do not record him saying, "I am tired," or "I am in pain," though he was tired and in pain. His most urgent outcry was "I thirst."

We have had recent reminders of the desperate thirst of suffering people. Television images show thousands of people in the path of war besieging the conquerors for an immediate drink and all but demanding that supplies of water be the first priority after the shooting. Even many of us in our luxury, far from battles and destruction, carry bottles of water to slake thirst hourly.

Of course, Jesus was thirsty. The dying always are. Nurses ministering on battlefields, rescuers reaching fallen mountain climbers, you when you have tended a loved one through to the final moments of life, know what water on parched lips means, as death strengthens its grip while the sufferer weakens.

"I thirst" was not a minor line in the drama of Gospel writers. Three of them record the scene, from different camera angles, and they come up with differing interpretations. This one by John stresses that Jesus said "I thirst" not just because he was understandably, desperately thirsty, but to fulfill the scripture.

No one knows which particular scripture this fulfills. The Bible has many references to the dry mouth, the tongue cleaving to the roof of the mouth, the dryness that leaves one at the door of death or drops a person down to the dust of death. At this moment, the one who said he gave the water of life, who even is the water of life, who gives of himself so that no one need thirst, now thirsts and drinks the drink of death. Nothing having to do with his thirst appears accidentally in John's Gospel. It belongs to the central plot. This portion had its place in the pattern of his giving and receiving as he finishes his work and moves toward his death.

T. L. BARRETT

Many think that Jesus uttered these words because he wanted to demonstrate he was human—that in the midst of all he was enduring, he still had normal needs and desires. They see this as the basis for a larger belief: despite experiencing the trials and tribulations of life, human needs must still be met.

Here Jesus was attempting to show that there were at least some in that angry mob who were merciful. In those times, depending on the seriousness of the crime, vinegar and gall was used as an anesthetic to lessen the pain of crucifixion. So when Jesus was offered the vinegar and gall, it was done in order to reduce his suffering.

There are some willing to "dip the sponge in the vinegar and gall" for you too, my friends, so that whatever agony you are experiencing can be endured more easily. But what about when *others* are suffering? Will *you* be among those who will lessen *their* pain, even when being merciful is inconvenient?

JOHN SHEA

Knowing that all things were now accomplished, that the scripture might be fulfilled, Jesus said "I thirst."

It was not the first time. Once before in John's Gospel he thirsted. "Give me a drink," he asked the Samaritan woman. But by the end he had given her a drink and told his disciples that his food and drink was to do the will of his Father. And the will of the divine source is to connect all there is to divine love. And so he thirsts to make that connection, to be that channel, to become a flow of grace to every moment of crucifixion. His thirst is to become water to our parched throats, wine to the failing weddings of our lives.

When we are at our end, when our resources seem depleted, when our energies are wasted, when our opportunities are gone, when we reach in the air for we know not what, then he cries again, *"I thirst."*

And his unquenched thirst brings him to us. We are no longer alone. The connection is made, the channel is open. Love, invisible yet real, flows.

Until the end of history he cries *"I thirst"* and becomes the companion of every emptiness, the secret fullness of every lack, brother to our suffering, peace in our pain, love where least expected.

STAN GUTHRIE

How ironic that the God-man, who freely gave the living water of eternal life, should face his death thirsty. Christians believe that before the eternal Son of God came to earth to pay the penalty for our sin, he had no needs. He lived in perfect fellowship with the Father and the Holy Spirit. Yet here he was, skewered to a cross, his tongue cleaving to the roof of his mouth.

Jesus was not a spirit trapped in a shell. He was perfect man with an imperfect body, and now, before the Resurrection, his body betrayed him. How like us! Jesus knew firsthand the frustration, the agony of the physical. The writer to the Hebrews says of him, "For we do not have a high priest who is unable to sympathize with our weaknesses." Yes, until the end we will face physical pain, disability, and thirst.

But Jesus knows. More than that, suspended between heaven and earth, he has shown us how we should respond to our thirst as we await our own resurrection. Again, the writer of Hebrews says, "Let us fix our eyes on Jesus, the author and perfecter of our faith, who for the joy set before him endured the Cross, scorning its shame, and sat down at the right hand of the throne of God."

Peter J. Gomes

The Reformation preachers on the seven words from the Cross called this fifth word the word of suffering, and it is the only word where Jesus actually expresses human pain and need. Perhaps even more than the fourth word, with its cry of human dereliction and its sense of loss, this fifth word is the word we most understand. If the fourth word is the most theological of the seven, this fifth word is the most human.

It is no small point to note that Jesus' first miracle that he did at Cana of Galilee was to satisfy the real thirst of those wedding guests when the unthinkable had happened and the host had run out of wine. I have always loved that miracle for its earthy, practical, and sensual quality, and to spiritualize it into some metaphysical lesson is to cheat the drinkers and to deprive Jesus of the credit of doing something useful.

By the same token, to spiritualize this fifth word into a longing and desire for God while failing to take seriously the human suffering that it evokes is again to deny the humanity and reality of the Passion. I do not doubt that Jesus thirsted for God, but I also believe that he suffered the thirst of one who is dying. It is his statement of mortality, and the word is important because it allows those real human beings at the foot of the Cross to respond at a human level to the human tragedy before them. It is a word, the only word, I suggest, addressed to the earthly crowd gathered at Jesus' feet.

It is a statement of fact. It is also an invitation to respond. To state one's thirst is to invite someone to quench it. Suddenly, we are no longer mere bystanders, voyeurs, kibbitzers. We are invited, by implication and sympathy, into the narrative. If we are looking for a place of resonance, of response, this is it. Jesus does not do his kingly death scene in silence or alone. We are now invited in.

> What can I give him, poor as I am?
> If I were a shepherd, I would bring a lamb.
> If I were a wise man, I would do my part;
> Yet, what I can I give him: give my heart.

DOROTHY MCRAE-MCMAHON

I thirst,
like a vulnerable seed
waiting under the parched farmland earth
for the rain to release me to life.

I thirst,
like the one who grieves the loss of its loves
in the deathly betrayals
which leech away the waters of hope.

I thirst,
like a nation longing for the generosity of its old soul
as it watches its life drying up and dying in meanness.

I thirst,
like the one whose spirit flies free in truth
while its body groans and weeps in the bleeding
from the costliness of its fight.

I thirst,
not for the sweet easy drink of denials,
nor for the sour wine offered by those who would call me from my path,
but for the holy water of risen life.

David Tracy

In John's Gospel—and John alone—every significant action and word of his victorious Jesus is heavy with symbolic meaning. For John, one must not only narrate the common passion story of this unsubstitutable Jesus. One must also stop, meditate, hear the often musical rhythm of the text, see the iconic power of Jesus' every word and deed. Even the lifting up of the Cross, the great scandal of Christianity, becomes in John, and John alone, in sign of the triumph, the beauty, the glory of God disclosed in this Jesus the Christ, as Christ returns to the Father and releases The Spirit upon the world.

Even the troubling words "I thirst" of John's Jesus force the hearer-reader not to dwell only in the stark realism of the words but also to move, in meditation, with John—to move ahead in time and back in space. Ahead, in time, to the flowing of the water and blood of the lanced corpse of the dead Jesus as his Spirit goes forth, in water and blood, to all. Back, in space, as the reader cannot forget, in hearing the words "I thirst" that this Jesus, now thirsty with the dry tongue of approaching death, earlier promised that those who drank of the water he would give would never thirst; back further yet in time and space to the waters of Exodus—the parting, rushing Red Sea and the thirst of the Israelites in the desert for forty years; back further yet to the pure water of Eden and, in and through the water imagery to see the Cross of Christ as the cosmic tree of all ancient religions: the tree whose branches reach to the heavens even as its roots plunge down into the healing, nourishing water held by earth.

The symbolism of John, even in the words of his Jesus "I thirst" is unmistakable to any attentive reader of John's rhythmic, meditative, iconic account of the death of Jesus.

And yet—the words of Jesus "I thirst" are not merely symbolic. "I thirst" is the cry of a dying man whose mouth is parched in the moments left from his approaching death—a death of shame and tortured pain. The cry of Jesus in John—"I thirst"—disrupts even John's profoundly symbolic and all too continuous account with a moment of unmistakably human—all too human—pain. Jesus thirsts. And those of us who, in Kierkegaard's accurate words, hear these words of Jesus on the Cross, do not presume to call ourselves Christians. We are rather those who would like to become Christians. We thirst. For our souls may be too small for real Christianity; our minds may be too parched; our use of Christian symbols too familiar; our longings for release too real, not to hear the words of this Jesus—our Jesus—in their awe-full poignancy: "I thirst."

David Neff

Jesus suffered horribly. To his followers and foes alike, it was unthinkable that the Messiah descended from David should suffer so. And yet his followers came to believe that this Messiah of David's stock was not only destined to recapitulate King David's glorious reign, but first to suffer as David suffered: abandonment, rejection, and, yes, even thirst.

To Jesus' followers, two Psalms of David recorded particularly rich parallels to Jesus' sufferings—numbers 22 and 69—and they both mention the thirst of a desperate man. It was not just Jesus' *thirst* that grabbed their attention. That was unremarkable. Rather it was the drink he was offered.

The Psalmist wrote: *"They gave me vinegar for my thirst,"* showing how his enemies scorned him. But in the hands of Jesus' executioners, this mixture of sour wine and myrrh was actually a small mercy designed both to quench thirst and to dull pain. And to the Gospel writer, this small charity was also a divine sign.

> Later, knowing that all was now completed, and *so that the Scripture would be fulfilled*, Jesus said, "I thirst."

But Jesus' thirst is also laced with irony:

> His executioners' act of mercy is linked to a Psalm about scorn and rejection.
> His body's compelling sense of thirst says, drink and live. Yet Jesus knows that he will die.
> The one who promised, "If anyone is thirsty, let him come to me and drink. . . . Streams of living water will flow from within him."—*that* person is now dying of thirst.

The life and death of Jesus are full of the most painful ironies. And so is God's world, a world riddled with contradiction. But it is also permeated with hope for a future in which all contradictions will be resolved, a future made possible by the one who endured the supreme contradiction for the sins of the world.

GROVER A. ZINN

Until now Jesus' words have focused our attention on others. Now this cry turns our gaze toward him, toward his physical suffering. He calls for nourishment, for water. And his cry is met not with compassion, but with heartless mockery as a sponge with vinegar is thrust toward his mouth.

One cannot hear this cry without recalling the times that Jesus responded to the thirst of others: the physical and spiritual thirst of the Samaritan woman at the well; the celebratory thirst of the guests at the wedding in Cana of Galilee; the thirst, again physical and spiritual, of crowds who heard him preach in Galilee; the cup of the Last Supper.

"I thirst"—words from the Cross; words heard in the midst of drought-stricken lands, in the poverty of inner cities, in the midst of wars. "I thirst"—words of spiritual emptiness heard in urban centers, in green groves, and on barren plains. Perhaps our greatest challenge is to find the deep wells of physical and spiritual nourishment that will slake the thirst of a wounded and weary world.

EVELYN VARBONCOEUR

Lord, why speak this word—"I thirst"—with your last breath?
Don't you know that the last words of the dying
Are etched in the memories of the living?
Are pondered in their hearts?
Are cherished as reflecting the full stature of the life of the dying one?

Ah—could it be that this is your intent?
Could it be that this word is a parable,
As were so many words spoken during your life?

Those of us who were with you
Have heard you speak this word before—
To the woman of Samaria.
And your thirst became in her
"a fountain of living water leaping up to eternal life."
Is this your intent now?
To make known to us this soul-thirst of yours,
This God-sized soul-thirst?

Once again—in your last breath
You cry out your thirst—this time to us
So that for all ages
Your thirst might again become a fountain of living water
In us.

Let this word be etched in our memories
Pondered in our hearts
Cherished as reflecting the full stature of your life.

When he took the wine,
Jesus said,

"IT IS FINISHED!"

And having bowed his head,
he gave over the spirit.

JOHN 19:30

Raymond E. Brown

The last word of Jesus in the Gospel of John is unlike that in any other Gospel: not a cry of anguish like *"My God, my God, why have you forsaken me?"* in Mark and Matthew; not a cry of loving trust like *"Father into your hands I commend my spirit,"* as in Luke, but a cry of victory. The Jesus of John is one who said, *"I lay down my life; I take it up again; no one takes it from me."* The crucified Jesus has decided that now is the time to lay it down, now is the time to die. He has conquered the world and cast down its Prince; he has gathered together at the foot of the Cross a community of those whom the Father has given him, personified in his mother and the beloved disciple; he has fulfilled the Scriptures. In other words, the Jesus of John has accomplished everything that the Father has given him to do. And so he can affirm with triumph, *"It is finished!"*

Whereas in the other Gospels Jesus lets go the spirit or breathes it out, expiring, in John Jesus gives it over—gives over his Spirit to that community of his own at the foot of the Cross. He had promised that if he departed, the Paraclete Spirit would come, and so his death is not only a victorious conclusion but also a beginning. Jesus has laid down his life for his sheep, so that through his Spirit that he gives over to them they might have life and have it more abundantly.

GILBERT C. MEILAENDER

"It is finished!" Jesus says. Ask the biblical scholars, and they will tell you that in John's Gospel these words are a cry of victory. And so, no doubt, they are. But how can we hear in them the sound of triumph?

I have watched my wife "laboring," as we say, to give birth to a child. The labor seems to go on and on—and then, suddenly, it is finished. The end of this labor is new life—a fulfillment that makes it all worthwhile.

This past December I watched my father die—"laboring," as we say, just to draw a breath for the last several days of his life. That labor also seems to go on and on—and then, suddenly, it too is finished. But where is the fulfillment that makes it all worthwhile, that makes it a victory? This labor just seems to end.

Can it be that the "labor" of our lives, which one day for us too may become the labor just to draw a breath . . . can it be that this "labor," when it is finished, has a point? An end that is fulfillment and victory?

To the eyes of faith the laborings of our lives are enfolded within that great labor of the man on the Cross. And faith gives rise to hope—hope that, in and through his labor, when we draw our last breath and say "It is finished!" those words may mark not just an end, but also a fulfillment and a victory.

ALISON BODEN

It *was* finished, wasn't it? It was completely and decisively finished by that cross. Those crossbeams! Nailed to them was the hope of the people. All the teaching, all the healing, all the anticipation of a time that would be so different from their own. It was finished.

Rome had won. Its brutal occupation was entrenched. No messiah to speak truth to power. No prophets left to speak of peace and an end to violence. No seers left to proclaim that love is stronger than hate. No Chosen One left to tell the people that there is more love in God than sin in us.

It is finished indeed: all our hopes for a day when "justice and righteousness will kiss," all our dreams of the day when the poor will be filled with good things and the meek will inherit the earth. It is finished: all our plans for a society where equity and harmony will reign. It is finished: all our prayers for a day when God will be all in all.

But what was finished? Was it love, hope, faith, justice? Was it the power of God? No—as he breathed his very last, Jesus saw it, he saw what was finished and proclaimed its end. It was sin that was finished. It was death itself. It was the stranglehold of human greed and envy and hate that makes us choose not life but death. Finished is the hunger for power that eclipses our thirst for righteousness. Evidence is all around that these things thrive among us, but they are vanquished already.

They are finished, for we are redeemed. The last will be first and the first will be last. Heaven is opened. From the Cross, he could see it all laid before him. It is finished. And it has all just begun!

JEAN BETHKE ELSHTAIN

Joy and sorrow mingle. A good and faithful servant has gone home: a carpenter, God's only begotten son, had pleaded: let this cup pass from me. But he drank the dregs to the last drop. God's judgment on the world would not be denied. Christ's earthly sojourn ended in the same death meted out to traitors and to criminals. It was finished, only to begin.

Centuries later another faithful servant met a cruel end. As he was summoned to his execution, anti-Nazi martyr and theologian Dietrich Bonhoeffer told those near him, as he handed one his Bible, "This is the end. For me, the beginning of life." It was finished, only to begin.

A clutch of memories from childhood, snatches of half-forgotten words and images. A funeral, one of my first. My paternal grandfather, a heart attack. My father's grim face. My mother's tears. My grandmother's stunned silence. The pastor, speaking of a Christian life well lived. My grandfather, another carpenter, had collapsed as he worked on the beams of a new addition to Our Savior's Lutheran Church. He died in the church in which he was now sent forth to be buried, recalled to his God. I heard the words, "Well done, thou good and faithful servant." For him too, it was finished, only to begin.

Edgar T. Thornton

The Gospels have preserved for all time words spoken by Jesus on Calvary. Their meaning provided a wide pattern of concern for those who gathered in the crowd that day. For some of the Roman guards, His final cry was that of a dying criminal who had received His just punishment. Other soldiers who witnessed the event were caught up with a feeling that Jesus must have been the Son of God. The followers of Jesus were broken-hearted and chilled with a sense of failure. Still others wondered about the outcome of their own lives when Jesus uttered those words, "It is finished!"

What was "finished" when Jesus made His pronouncement that day? Was He referring to the end of His suffering on the Cross? Was His announcement an admission that His plan to save the world had been defeated by the power of Rome?

No, the cry of Jesus as He hung on the Cross was not about failure or suffering or pain. Jesus was giving a shout of victory! He represented a Power far greater than Rome or her mighty army. The Man on that Cross was God's Son. God never fails. Jesus fulfilled the purpose of God for the plan of mankind's redemption when He said, "It is finished!"

His cry was not the bitterness that comes with pain and sorrow and disappointment. He came on earth to complete a divine mission. He had done all that could be done to make God known to man and to identify Him with men. He had come to bring the abundant life for mankind. God's ultimate purpose—to reach out to His people and to redeem them— was completed. All of this was secured by Jesus in His deeds and teachings, but much more in His self-giving death upon the Cross. "For God so loved the world that He gave His only Son so that everyone who believed in Him may not perish but may have eternal life."

TOMÁS BISSONNETTE

Observe carefully. Jesus does not say "**I** am finished." He says, *"It is finished!"*—his work, what he needed to do. Yet his life was cut short, and his work seemed to be in shambles. The world had not been transformed. The reign of the Spirit was hardly evident. His apostles were far from understanding his work, or their part in it. Still, Jesus confidently announces, "It is finished!"

Every day he had given, not just *of* himself, but himself—completely and fully to what he understood the Father wanted. Confidently then, he could leave the work to those who followed—his way of saying that we who live with imperfection and limitations at the eventide of our lives have a right to announce, "It is finished." We have done our job. We leave the rest of the work to those who follow, even though they little understand what we are about. If only each of us at the end of life could say, "I have given myself to the mission with which I believe God entrusted me. Faithfully and happily I have done my best. I can confidently die with Christ, even in the worst of circumstances, even strung up on a cross." Paschal joy invades the suffering of the Cross—while the Easter mystery gives life and joy and inspires Christian optimism in the face of death.

Jarrett Kerbel

They said she had a terrible headache. The lights were turned off and the blinds drawn tight in her room where she would lay in her bed day after day. Her four-year-old only daughter, still wearing stitches and bandages herself, knew with a child's instinct that her mother's suffering was more than a headache. The family moved as lightly as ghosts around the darkened house.

Ninety years later that same daughter told me how her mother had tried to hold her son's brains inside his skull as a borrowed car lurched across the rutted tracks to the nearest doctor. The accident happened at a hunting camp. During a game of cowboys and Indians one brother had leveled a rifle at the youngest, who was in her sister's arms. He didn't know it was loaded.

One day well after the accident, the sewing machine began to hum and peck in the darkened bedroom. Peeking in, the daughter saw her mother sewing a gold-braid cross on a field of white satin. This work of grief was a memorial to be used in the children's processions at church.

135

As a pastor I accompany individuals and families through death. I know the finality of death and the need to acknowledge that someone has been lost, that some cherished person will never be with us again. I also know the finality of unfinished business; the messy loose ends of wounded relationships that are left tender with frustration when the person who seems to hold the key to reconciliation is gone.

In his solidarity with our humanity, Jesus did not skip or cheat the ultimate loss. He suffered the human condition to the end: *"It is finished!"* Our grieving is not unfaithful; it is a witness to the sacred span of human living and dying.

We who live on the other side of Easter are blessed to know that *"It is finished!"* is part of a larger story. The challenge of these words, however, is whether or not we can cradle the finitude of our existence in the hope that we will never finally be lost to God. It does no justice to our humanity to erase the sorrow of our frailty by trying to forget it or gloss it away with premature visions of heaven. Skipping or cheating this reality only diminishes our capacity for compassion and solidarity as modeled most perfectly by Jesus.

JOAN BROWN CAMPBELL

"It is finished!"—words of pathos, finality. Yes, but also words of resolve—a complete task. Jesus, son of God came to earth as man, cannot overcome death. For the crucifixion to mean anything, it must be real. Death must overcome even Jesus. Real tears must be shed, real bodies broken.

We dare not rush to the glory of Easter morning seeking a too easy release from the tragedy of the death of Jesus. Human beings do face evil and are overcome by it. That is what makes it evil. Light is only a gift because it relieves us from the depth of darkness. In the crucifixion, we engage the most human act of all—dying a human death. Jesus dies with the total dignity of one who has put himself in God's hands. Jesus cannot overcome death. Death cannot overcome God.

Easter is God's great gift—the sure knowledge that finally life does overcome death. But we hold in our hearts both that gift and the reality of the limits of our earthly pilgrimage. God's challenge to us is in our living, for it is in our daily lives and struggles that we overcome death. It is every day that we bear witness to God's gift of love. And when we have run with perseverance the race set before us, then, like Jesus, we may lay down our faithful lives and say, *"It is finished!"*

ANDREW M. GREELEY

There comes a time when we must let go. We must give up being a baby to become a kid. We must abandon being a kid so that we might be a teen. We must relinquish high school so that we can go to college. We must some day eventually stop being a student and get a job. We must give up the freedom of the single state to marry, to adjust to a spouse, and then to adjust to children. We must some day permit the children to be free so that they can be adults on their terms, not ours. We must give up health and perhaps independence as we grow older. Eventually we must give up life itself.

At each of these times of surrender in our lives we must trust. We must trust God, other human beings, and ourselves. Dying is not only the end of living; it is part of living. Each new yielding opens up the possibility of something new that is both frightening and appealing. We have no choice in the matter. Every day we must yield our spirit to grace. We can do so stubbornly, reluctantly, with protests and complaints. We can curse the dimming of the light. Or we can go gracefully into the night as Jesus did, firm in the knowledge that it is safe to say *"It is finished!"*

Francis George

The baptism by John and the temptation in the desert, the calling of the disciples and the proclamation of the Kingdom, the healing and the teaching, the institution of the Eucharist and the structuring of the Church, the betrayal and condemnation, the scourging and the crowning, the crucifixion and desolation—all is finished; but nothing is lost, for all is fulfilled in Christ.

Like God looking at the work of creation and declaring it finished before resting on the seventh day, Jesus on the Cross looks at the work of redemption and calls it finished before he goes to his death. There will be no second Savior, but Christ will send the Spirit to continue this work until He comes again in glory.

Then, at that coming, the world will hear this word for the third and last time: *"It is finished!"*

Jesus cried out with
a loud voice saying,

**"FATHER, INTO YOUR HANDS
I COMMEND MY SPIRIT."**

And having said this,
he breathed his last.

LUKE 23:46

Martin Luther King Jr.

I can hear Jesus himself, standing amid the agony and darkness of Good Friday, standing amid the darkness of the Cross. And out of the pain and the agony and the darkness of that cross, we hear a voice saying, *"Into thy hands I commend my spirit."* And then we can hear him saying, "Not *my* will, but *thy* will be done." Now you got to learn that, my friends, and when you learn that, you can stand up amid any condition, because you know that God is with you, no matter what happens. You can stand up amid despair. You can stand up amid persecution. You can stand up amid disappointment. You can stand up even amid death. But you don't worry because you know God is with you.

And so, I'm going away this morning—I don't know about you—but I'm going away determined that wherever he leads me, I will follow. I will follow him to the Garden. I will follow him to the Cross if he wants me to go there. I will follow him to the dark valleys of death if he wants me to go there. Not *my* will, but *thy* will be done! And when you can cry that, you stand up amid life with an exuberant joy. You know that God walks with you. Even though you walk through the valley of the shadow of death, you know that God is there. Even though you stand amid the giant shadow of disappointment, you don't despair, because you know God is with you.

FRANCIS GEORGE

Jesus, at twelve, found himself in his Father's house in Jerusalem. His Father was with him in the garden of agony as Jesus asked that the cup be taken from him. His Father listened to Jesus praying for forgiveness for those nailing him to the Cross. Taken by force into his enemies' hands, Jesus now surrenders himself freely into his Father's hands.

Only Jesus can surrender his life and take it up again. No one has ever died as Jesus died. No one has ever entered so completely into utter helplessness.

No one else can surrender the very Spirit of life, the Spirit who descended upon Mary at Jesus' conception in her womb, the Spirit who came upon Jesus in the River Jordan, the Spirit who sustained Jesus' ministry in Galilee and Judea. The Spirit returns to the Father so that Jesus, risen from the dead, can send this same Spirit to give life to the Church, which is his body here and now. All is surrendered, given freely, without reserve, so that everything given can be shared.

Lord of life and Lord of death, bring us with you to your Father and ours. Amen.

ALISON BODEN

These were the last words of a dying man: into your hands, gracious God, I place my spirit. They were the words of a man dying not of disease or accident, but premeditated murder—execution. Betrayed, convicted on the flimsiest of evidence, abandoned by his friends and left absolutely alone—under such circumstances, how did he dare to say, "into your hands I commend my spirit?"

It was possible only because he had been saying it every day of his life. Jesus had trusted God with his spirit every day that he had drawn breath. When the crowds around him were growing and were adoring, when everyone in the region wanted just to touch the fringe of his cloak, he placed all of himself in the hands of God. When the people of his own hometown, the folks he'd grown up with, who had known him since he was a boy, wouldn't accept what he had become and drove him from town in a murderous mob, Jesus placed all of himself in the hands of God. When his killers circled closer and closer in the garden and he prayed to be spared, he placed all of himself in the hands of God. With his last, suffocating breath on the Cross, he knew he could place all of himself in the hands of God.

Good ole Monday, boring lunch meeting; Tuesday, dentist appointment; Wednesday, spreadsheets beyond number; Thursday, challenge from a colleague to a decision painfully arrived at; Friday, fight over breakfast that clouds the day. "Into your hands I commend my spirit."

Monday, spiritual epiphany in a lunch meeting; Tuesday, noticed first buds on tulip tree; Wednesday, felt the strongest, gentlest, holy accompaniment while walking down the street; Thursday, was privileged to be taken into the deepest confidence of an acquaintance; Friday, figured out that being the perfect lover, parent, student, friend, is not what matters. "Into thy hands I commend my spirit."

Let us learn from the last words of a dying man that in every minute we live (and in the moment we die) the open hands of love are waiting to receive our spirits, waiting to receive the whole of our lives.

DONALD L. PARSON

The final utterance of Christ from the Cross exposes a principle to be practiced and a prayer to be prayed. This statement reveals that Jesus died as He lived, trusting the wisdom of His Father, praying, and speaking scripture.

I am inspired by these words, so sparse of quantity, yet so abundant in implications. These words are not just reserved for last rites, funeral sermons, and Holy Week meditations. The final shout of Christ is a spiritual endowment for moments of uncertainty. It is a statement which sentences us to a lifetime of Godly wisdom and divine power.

These words liberate us, to freely expect beyond deadlines and death dates, that possibilities await us. Father into thy hands is a statement of reconciliation. If you'll remember, the fourth word asks a heart-wrenching question: Why hast thou forsaken me? However, the seventh word leaves no doubt that there is oneness between the Father and the Son.

Whether facing the death of a dream, the failure of an endeavor, the end of a shattered relationship, or the termination of a well-lived life, Jesus teaches us from the Cross to say "Into thy hands I commend my spirit." All that I am I place in the secure sanctuary of your hands. These words provide us with hope beyond our hopelessness. They say, in fact, that with human efforts I am crucified, but in thy hands I shall know resurrection.

Peter J. Gomes

The seventh word of Jesus makes the transition from this world to the next, and does so in confidence of the Father's love and trustworthiness. A commendation is not as we usually think of it, an award or even a reward. It is in this sense an act of trust and confidence that the God who has brought us thus far along the road will not abandon us now. It is into the hands of a loving God, the God who created and sustained him, that Jesus now commends himself. He enters into rest, not the mere absence of labor and stress, but into the presence of serenity and tranquility itself. As we sing in the hymn called *Victory*, "The strife is o'er, the battle done . . ."

There is an old saying that says all of life is meant to be lived in order to teach us how to die. Most of us resist that. Life is meant to teach us how to live, we say, and living well is the best revenge. We hold on to life. We fight for it. We don't like the alternative, and death is the villain that ruins the place. We, however, are people who are born so that we may know how to die. Our only destiny is our end, we all know that, no matter how life-enhancing and death-denying we are. The Prayer Book tells us that in the midst of life we are in death, and that is true.

So, on Good Friday, and at this seventh word, we must be reminded, forcibly if necessary, of what distinguishes us from the natural cycle of things. We believe that not only has Jesus hallowed life by his presence in it, but also that now he hallows death by his presence there as well, and where he goes, we need not fear to follow. That is what St. Paul means when he says, "O death where is thy sting? O grave where is thy victory?"

This last word the Reformer Preachers of Good Friday called the word of Triumph. It was not triumphant in the sense that Jesus cheated either his murderers or death itself. It was a word of triumph in that Jesus went not into death, but beyond death, and into the arms of God's eternity. As we follow him in life, so too do we follow him in death, just as we are, knowing that where he is we need not fear to be or go.

FRANK BRENNAN

In Luke's Gospel, Jesus makes three statements at the time of his crucifixion. First he asks the father to forgive those responsible. Then he consoles the good thief. Finally in the words of the psalmist he cries aloud to the father, *"Father, into your hands I commend my spirit."*

Forgiveness, consolation, and surrender. The challenge to any of us committed to living life to the full, committed to standing in solidarity against all the odds, committed to loving until death do us part, committed to life beyond death, to glory beyond suffering, to justice beyond the given distribution and the entrenched disorder of our world. The surrender of Jesus empties us of pride and grounds our hope. Whether nailed down, strung up, or just stretched to the limits of our fears, Lord, we ask for the generosity to forgive, the good grace to console, and the faith to surrender, not early or in cowardice, but having given our all and in your good time.

JOHN C. ORTBERG

Into your hands . . .

A two-year-old girl stands by the side of a pool. "Jump," her father says. She is filled with fear. She is quite certain that if she jumps, she will die. But she knows these hands. She trusts these hands. So she jumps. She abandons herself to her father. In between the jumping and the landing, everything in the world depends on these hands.

The history of this earth, in a way we don't fully understand, comes to this one moment. A lone figure is stretched out on a cross between heaven and earth, life and death. All the fear and loneliness of the human race has been somehow poured out on him. He has been asked by his father to do that which he most dreads.

But he knows these hands. He trusts these hands. So he says a prayer. He says it now because he has said it every day of his life. It's not the kind of prayer you hold in reserve.

Into your hands . . .

Each of us will stand on that edge one day: in a hospital room, maybe; or a convalescent ward; or some unsuspected place. We too will taste fear. None of us knows all about what comes next—not really; we all live between the jumping and the landing.

So Christ invites us to make his prayer our own. He offers these words as the final gift of his earthly life; the last, best prayer of humankind:

"Father, into your hands I commend my spirit."

ASHOK G. BHATT

This is a declaration of The Eternal Truth by Jesus Christ for the benefit of all mankind. This profound declaration transcends all the narrow definitions of religion. Jesus Christ, The Realized Soul, The Master, has realized The Eternal Truth:

That it is THE ETERNAL, "THE FATHER," the omnipresent, omnipotent, omniscient CAUSE that manifests, individually and collectively, as this universe of things and beings;

That this universe of things and beings are nothing but an effect of that CAUSE;

That without that CAUSE, no effect is possible;

That this ETERNAL BEING, the CAUSE, wills the creation, sustenance, and disappearance of this ever-changing universe of things and beings;

That HE is The Owner, The Doer, The Enjoyer, and we are His Instruments, acting only at HIS will;

That our Ego, our Spirit, is nothing but HIS individualized reflection;

That as we are made in HIS image, HE commands us to live as the children of Divinity, to see THE LORD in every thing and being, to give unconditional love to everyone, to live harmoniously with each other, to be good and do good, to help others and thank them for that privilege;

That HE is The ETERNAL without second, that HE only IS. That everything else in this ephemeral, ever-changing universe appears TO BE.

The Master thus cries out with joy, *"Father, into your hands I commend my spirit."*

ARTHUR M. BRAZIER

The key word in the last sentence spoken by our Lord is "commend." This verb can mean one of two things. It can represent someone who is worthy of notice or regard, such as a soldier who is given a commendation for bravery. It can also mean to commit, to entrust, to put oneself in the care of another. The latter is the true sense of Jesus' last utterance from the Cross. It was with this meaning in mind that Shakespeare wrote in his last will and testament, "I commend my soul into the hands of God, my Creator, hoping and assuredly believing through the only merits of Jesus Christ, my Saviour, to be made partaker of life everlasting." It is because of what Jesus did at Calvary that Shakespeare and all other believers in Christ can have that blessed assurance.

Jesus was able to commend his human spirit into the hands of the Father because he had finished the work the Father had given him to do. While Jesus performed many miracles of healing the sick, opening the eyes of the blind and casting out demons, these acts were not the reason he came into the world. These supernatural acts only served as his credentials, establishing the fact that he was indeed the son of God. The true reason he came into the world was to be the anti-type of the lamb that was sacrificed when God delivered Israel out of the house of bondage in Egypt. Jesus was God's lamb who suffered for us. Just as the children of Israel placed their faith in the slain lamb in Egypt, so do we place our faith in God's lamb, Jesus Christ.

Have faith in Jesus, who shed his blood on the cruel Cross so that our sins might be forgiven. Have faith in Jesus so we can take wing and soar from the foul and lonesome valley of sin to the majestic slopes of fellowship with God. Have faith in Jesus so we can breathe the pure air of sanctification and holiness.

After having suffered, after having been reviled, after having been beaten with the Roman lash, after having his tender brow pierced with a crown of thorns, after having been nailed to the Cross, his work having been done in perfect obedience, he uttered these final words that seemed so full of peace and serenity: *"Father, into thy hands I commend my spirit."*

149

GROVER A. ZINN

With the last gasp of breath from his dying body, Jesus utters these words. As with the first word from the Cross, he reaches beyond himself, to the God whom he calls "Father." He asks nothing for himself; not for deliverance, not for pity, not for release from pain. Instead, at the last moment of bodily life, he places himself, full of trust, into the hands of God.

How difficult it is to take whatever we have struggled to complete in a lifetime or a moment and place it into the hands of another. Yet this is the final secret that Jesus imparts to us: only the strength of faith leads us through the darkness of death, toward the light of everlasting love.

ANDREW M. GREELEY

We all die. Perhaps from a jab of a bayonet in our belly, or poison gas pouring through a shower nozzle, or an exploding jet, or the crash of a truck, or a thundering commuter train against our car, or a bullet in our brain, or a ruptured heart. Or death may take us more slowly. A lingering stroke, a slow-moving cancer, failing lungs, collapsing kidneys. However we die, it is in terror, whether the terror be momentary or long.

Our lives, our failed dreams, our blighted hopes, our mistakes, our failures, our sins, our moments of joy, our interludes of love, our seasons of happiness—all are snuffed out.

We die by ourselves or surrounded by family and friends, but we still all die alone, we face the terror alone, we enter the darkness alone, we give up all that we have and all that we are—alone.

But not quite alone.

151

When Jesus died he promised us, in effect, that when it came time for us to go down into the valley of death he would go with us. He promised us that he knows what it is like and he will aid us and protect us on this most dangerous of journeys.

But not only Jesus. Our faith tells us that the God who is with Jesus and in Jesus will be with us too. God walks down the steep and dark road into the valley of death. We are not alone after all.

The seven last words of Jesus are also *our* seven last words—the words of terror and loneliness, of fear and horror, of despair and final surrender as we complete our journey and perhaps begin a new one.

Yet they are not words without hope. Jesus knew that the God who was with him even among the dead would vindicate him, that he would return from the valley of death to live again. Jesus promises us that he will hold our hand on that trip down—and on the trip back.

On Good Friday we ask whether we can face death with hope, even as Jesus did when he said, *"Father, into your hands I commend my spirit."*

THE EARTHQUAKE

Behold! The veil of the temple was torn in two from top
to bottom. And the earth quaked, and the rocks were split,
and the graves were opened, and many bodies of
the saints who had fallen asleep were now raised.

An angel of the Lord descended from heaven, and
rolled back the stone from the door and sat on it.
His countenance was like lightning, and his clothing
as white as snow. And the guards shook for fear of him,
and became like dead men. But the angel answered and
said to the women: "Do not be afraid, for I know that you
seek Jesus who was crucified. He is not here, for he is risen,
as he said. Come, see the place where the Lord lay. And go
quickly and tell his disciples that he is risen from the dead."

Now when the centurion and those with him who
were guarding Jesus saw the earthquake and the
things that had happened, they feared greatly,
saying, "Truly this was the son of God!"

MATTHEW 27:51–54; 28:2–7

RICHARD YOUNG

EARTHQUAKE INTRODUCTION[1]

There is little left to this narrative on the hill, on that horrible day which we now call Good Friday. Jesus is still hanging from the Cross, still hanging onto life by a thread, having said all that needed to be said. He now awaits death—a death that not only marks the end of his suffering, but which many believers also see as the passage to life. For them, the earthquake that immediately followed Jesus' death is not just a natural phenomenon, but an inviting symbol of the spiritual upheaval caused by this passage. For others, the symbolism is more graphic: the earthquake is an "act of God" that represents the Father's violent protest of the death of his son.

With Jesus' death we have now reached a moment of overwhelming significance—a moment dramatized by the shuddering and rumbling earth suddenly sundering beneath us. No account is more vivid than the Gospel according to Matthew . . .

JOHN SHEA

EARTHQUAKE INTRODUCTION

Now that the man in whom the One Word Became Many Words is silent, St. Matthew writes: "Behold, the veil of the temple was torn in two from top to bottom."

The forbidding curtain of the temple that separated God from people is torn in two—from top to bottom. The rip is permanent and complete. It cannot be repaired. Behold it. Through this torn and flapping curtain the wind of the Spirit freely flows. God is released into life.

St. Matthew continues: "And the earth quaked, and rocks were split, and graves were opened, and many bodies of the saints who had fallen asleep were raised."

Now that the man in whom the One Word Became Many Words is silent, the earth begins to speak. A long muteness is over. Its utterance begins with interior convulsions; a force in the center of the universe erupts. This force rumbles upward, parting the sealed lips of the surface, splitting rocks so flesh can emerge. Awakened to its Source, the earth speaks. Its word is resurrection.

But there is more. Now that the man in whom the One Word Became Many Words is silent, other voices begin to speak. Jesus has untied the knot in the tongues of the children of God, and all who speak acknowledge him. His silence is the beginning of symphony.

St. Matthew tells us: "Now when the centurion and those with him who were guarding Jesus saw the earthquake and the things that had happened, they feared greatly, saying: truly this was the son of God!"

THE WORDS
AND THE MUSIC

RICHARD YOUNG[1]

The accompanying CD #2 contains recorded examples, each on a separate track. They should be played, when indicated, as one reads this chapter.

BACKGROUND, FORMAT, AND THE INTRODUCTION

By 1785 Franz Joseph Haydn's fame had spread throughout Europe. It is therefore not so surprising that he was contacted by the bishop of a church in the town of Cadiz, on the southern coast of Spain. The bishop wanted something special for Good Friday. But instead of a work that was *generally* inspired by the crucifixion of Jesus—of which there were already scores—he requested an instrumental piece that was *specifically* based on Jesus' seven final utterances from the Cross. Haydn, who was not only a devout Christian but appears to have had a surprisingly sophisticated understanding of theology, readily accepted. Religious conviction may not have been his sole motivation, however, since he must have realized that he would be reaching a much broader audience than ever before, well beyond the privileged upper class who attended his concerts and commissioned most of his music.

Composed in 1786, *The Seven Last Words of Christ* consists of seven slow *sonatas,* each based on one of Jesus' seven final utterances. Two additional movements frame these sonatas: a solemn *Introduction* and a fiery *finale,* entitled *Il Terremoto,* which depicted the earthquake that followed Jesus' death. The work was first presented on Good Friday, 1787, in an austere setting that was completely dark, except for the glow from the wick of a single lamp, hung from above. Following the *Introduction,* the bishop recited the first of the Seven Last Words, which served as the basis for a short spoken meditation. The first of Haydn's sonatas was then played. Each of the remaining sections followed the same pattern: the bishop would introduce one of Jesus' final utterances, and the music that it inspired would immediately follow.

Haydn's masterpiece was conceived in a spirit of profound religious conviction. Despite its length and emotional urgency, it is a model of simplicity and sophistication. Above all, Haydn wanted it to be accessible to everybody, regardless of the listener's musical, religious, or cultural background. He wrote: "Each sonata, or movement, is expressed by purely instrumental music in such a way that even the most uninitiated listener will be moved to the very depths of his soul."

The work was originally scored for full orchestra. While these parts were being printed in 1787, Haydn crafted an alternate version for string quartet. Later that year, under Haydn's supervision, the publisher made a piano reduction of the orchestra score. Various arrangements for choir were also done, including one by the composer.

In the hands of a mere four string players, this music cannot achieve the volume and tonal diversity of a symphony orchestra or choir. Nevertheless, in the four-voice setting, with only one instrument on a part, it is imbued with a heightened intimacy that larger ensembles cannot possibly match. This music's emotional and psychological impact is best conveyed through the subtlest variations of timbre, voicing, rhythm, and tempo—techniques ideally suited to a string quartet. Therefore this simplest of all versions may indeed be the most affecting. No less compelling than its more grandiose cousins, it is inherently more personal.

Haydn considered *The Seven Last Words of Christ* one of his greatest works. In fact, he felt so personally identified with this music that when signing his name at the end of a letter he would often add his "musical autograph:" the five notes that correspond to the syllables *"Con-sum-ma-tum est,"* the notes which begin the movement inspired by Jesus' sixth word from the Cross, *"It is finished!"* (This musical autograph is reprinted on the very last page of this book.) But to hear the music by itself, however powerfully it stands alone, is to experience it in only part of its glory. Reunited with the words that served as its inspiration, it takes on a spiritual dimension rarely found in even the most profound compositions.

Listeners may have difficulty perceiving *The Seven Last Words of Christ* as a whole. If we are regarding a painting or a piece of sculpture, we are able to take it in all at once. We can do so in a general way or we can focus on whatever details strike our fancy. And because we are not constrained in any way by the passage of time, we can also spend whatever moments we feel are necessary to linger on certain features. But with a piece of music, particularly such a large composition, this is impossible. Because a listener has no choice but to hear it unfolding little by little, note by note, he or she cannot simultaneously have an overview of its entirety. When studying a painting, one's eye can move from place to place. When reading a novel, one has the freedom to reread certain passages or even jump ahead. When regarding a sculpture, one can move around and view it from different angles to establish perspective. But when listening to music, one has no choice but to accept it on its own rather limited terms as it passes through time at its own predetermined pace. Sound has certain inherent limitations that composers wrestle with constantly. While it is certainly *directional,* and while it gives the impression of being *dimensional,* there is nothing about it that quite corresponds to the *three-dimensional* visual possibilities that are essential to our appreciation of sculpture. While we have "stereophonic" sound and "surround-sound," we do not have *multidimensional* sound, despite what the salesperson told you when you last shopped for loudspeakers. It is therefore up to composers to create the illusion of many dimensions—of "depth" and "breadth"—which they do through variations in volume, timbre, texture, and melodic, harmonic, and rhythmic activity.

Among the biggest challenges composers face are those posed by the limitations that necessarily exist in perceiving the unity of any piece of music. In *The Seven Last Words of Christ,* Haydn made some decisions early on that almost guarantee that its unity will be appreciated, consciously or subconsciously. First, the music is held together by the text that inspired it. Just as Jesus' seven last utterances have a narrative quality, so too do Haydn's settings of them. Second, since each of these settings is generally slow—*adagio, lento, grave, maestoso,* or *largo*—there is a unity of tempo and pace. The work proceeds at a very contemplative, meditative speed for the first eight movements until we run up against the *finale,* the shocking *Earthquake* movement.

Haydn's decisions, though, do little to solve the work's most significant problem: how to keep listeners from feeling that they are floating aimlessly on a vast and seemingly endless sea of slow movements. There are a couple of ways we can listen to this piece to help maintain our sense of where we are as we slowly proceed forward. One is to recognize that the movements—their opening phrases, at least—alternate between the minor and major modes. For instance, Haydn writes the *Introduction* in the key of D minor, which establishes the very serious character of the work. But the very next movement, *"Father, forgive them, for they know not what they do,"* is in B-flat major, which has a far more yielding and sunlit quality. As we move through the piece movement by movement, it is almost as if a window or a shutter opens and closes on the light. We go from dark to light, and back again, on a precisely alternating basis.

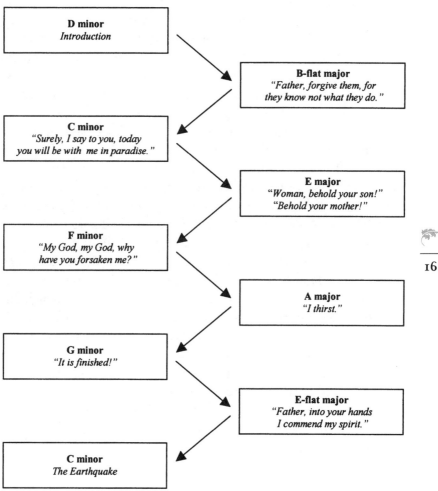

Another thing that is very helpful is to focus on Haydn's use of "signature" motifs, which in music are called *motives*. He begins each movement with a clearly identifiable two-, three-, or five-note motive, upon which he bases the rest of the music throughout the movement. [Grover Zinn elaborates on page 187.] Through a technique we call *motivic development,* he tinkers with these motives in much the same way the bishop at Cadiz meditated on the short written epigrams. So as we progress through these rather long and imposing sonatas, it is helpful to identify the motive, then follow its subsequent development. These motives thus serve not only as hooks on which to hang our hat, but also as a means to measure our progress through the piece.

The dark and dramatic *Introduction* opens with a five-note motive that includes a dotted figure, which gives it the character of a public piece. It is a call to worship, an encouragement to pay attention to what is coming. Not coincidentally, dotted rhythms show up often in "public music"—in national anthems, fanfares, and marches, for example. Immediately following this clarion call is a quiet and portentous interlude that introduces music that has a desperate and almost frenzied quality. A pulsating eighth-note figure emphasizes Jesus' desperation as he now hangs helplessly from the Cross. Even though the tempo is slow throughout, there is edge-of-the-chair drama in every note. Though this music is not programmatic—no particular script is here indicated—it encourages listeners to reflect on the events that immediately preceded the moments when Jesus uttered his Seven Last Words: The Last Supper. The agonizing anticipation in the Garden of Gethsemane. The betrayal by Judas. Jesus' arrest and trial before Pilate. The insults. The whippings. Jesus carrying his own cross up the hill to Calvary. The nails being hammered into his hands and feet. Listen now to this brief excerpt from the beginning of the *Introduction*.

TRACK 1

"FATHER, FORGIVE THEM, FOR THEY KNOW NOT WHAT THEY DO."

The very first words we hear from Jesus after he had been nailed to the Cross are not words of anger, vengeance, or self-pity. They are words of forgiveness. When we come to this part of the Good Friday story, we are inspired by Jesus' example—believers and nonbelievers alike. That is because every one of us has experience with forgiveness—sometimes bitter experience. We all know how very difficult it is to forgive someone who has deeply hurt us. We also know that it is not so easy to be the recipient of someone else's unconditional forgiveness, since this requires *us* to be unconditional forgivers when the tables are turned. So when we hear Jesus' first words from the Cross, we are filled with lofty inspiration and idealism. We say to ourselves, if this man could forgive the very people who were in the process of murdering him, shouldn't forgiveness come less hard for *us*? As we might expect, Haydn's music captures all of these high-minded sentiments. Listen now to the beginning of this movement, to music that is so yielding, so reconciling, and so forgiving.

TRACK 2

We have now come to the first of many challenges in this piece: *not all the music in this movement sounds like this!* About halfway through, we feel a knot beginning to form in our gut. Little by little, we sense anxiety, tension, and conflict. As we now listen to this excerpt, ask yourself, *why?*

TRACK 3

Whenever we have questions about the character of the music—why does it sound and feel the way it does?—the place to look for answers is not a musicology textbook, but rather, the particular scripture verses from the Bible that inspired this music. So let's examine this passage from Luke: *"Father, forgive them, for they know not what they do."* Here, it seems that forgiveness is somehow linked to ignorance. If you are ignorant enough, if you are clueless as to the consequences of your deeds or words, *then* you qualify for forgiveness! Peter Gomes has suggested elsewhere that this resembles our modern-day plea of temporary insanity—one of society's more divisive issues. It's like getting a "do-over" on the playground, a "get-out-of-jail-free" card in Monopoly, or a "mulligan" in golf. You can splash your golf ball into the pond or slice it into the woods and it doesn't matter, because with a "mulligan," it doesn't count. You get to continue as if it never happened. This seems all too good to be true—and in fact, it is. Ethicists from St. Augustine to Jean Bethke Elshtain remind us that it is not quite so simple as that. It's not as if there are no strings attached to forgiveness, no conditions that must first be met. So we have to get past our misleading first impressions and examine the scripture more carefully.

Just who are these executioners of Jesus, the ones for whom he is asking forgiveness? Are they really so ignorant? Historians like Father Raymond Brown inform us that they were neither naïve nor uninformed. They were not part of the criminal element. They knew the Ten Commandments. They understood that what they were doing was horribly wrong, yet they did it anyway. Wrapping themselves in virtue and righteousness, they were able to convince themselves and others that they were answering to a "higher authority," they were motivated by "the greater good." Gomes has warned that an excess of virtue is more dangerous than an excess of vice. This is because an excess of virtue is not subject to the same restraints of conscience. By doing the "wrong" thing for the "right" reasons, Jesus' executioners were in effect awarding themselves a "morality mulligan." Clearly, what we see here is no ordinary brand of ignorance. Gomes calls it a profound *ignorance of the soul.*

Throughout history, *these* kinds of people and *this* type of ignorance have been the most difficult to reconcile with an ethical and moral viewpoint. Martin Marty tells us that early Christian scribes were so repulsed by the idea that Jesus' executioners might be forgiven that they actually removed this portion of Luke's Gospel from their Bibles. Though we don't seem to mind this part of the story—indeed, we are *inspired* by it—we are troubled by the disquieting possibility that some of today's most repugnant individuals might be candidates for forgiveness.

Examples are all around us. Take the bomber of an abortion clinic. The usual profile is that of an adult male, middle to upper-middle class, well educated, a "family values" person, and someone who has fully considered the consequences of his actions. Most troubling of all is that he is usually a devout Christian whose faith motivates every aspect of his life. Since he generally shows little or no regret or remorse, one must assume that he would do it again if given the opportunity. He is compelled to act *because* of his religious convictions, not *in spite* of them. Regardless of our personal views on abortion, most of us see a bombing as clearly abhorrent behavior—the manifestation of the most twisted sort of zealotry. Does *this* sort of person deserve forgiveness?

How about Slobodan Milosovic and a host of other "ethnic cleansers?" (What an obscene euphemism that is!) How about all the warring parties in the Middle East? How about the terrorists responsible for 9/11 who justified their horrific atrocities not only by claiming that they are motivated by "the greater good," but by proclaiming that God is on their side? Should forgiveness be equally divided among *them*? It seems that the more closely we examine this very complicated and troubling question of forgiveness, the more we are filled with anxiety, tension, and conflict—*which, I submit, is the very same kind of anxiety, tension, and conflict that we hear in these portions of Haydn's music.*

Just look at what Haydn has done. In this serenely beautiful yet philosophically challenging movement, he has expressed not only our high-minded idealism when we first consider Jesus' forgiveness of his executioners, but also our complicated and conflicting emotions when we later ponder the ramifications of forgiveness in situations that more closely touch our own lives. Those who view good old Papa Haydn as merely the provider of quaint and light-hearted music for the powdered wig set might want to begin to revise their assessment.

"Surely, I say to you, today you will be with me in paradise."

This is the culminating line in the famous story of "the thief on the cross"—one of the most colorful and dramatic stories in the Bible. I suspect the reason why it is also one of the most endearing and enduring stories is because it's about each one of us. It's about those of us who have been believers all our lives. It's about those of us who have only recently become believers, perhaps under unusual circumstances. It's about those of us who have never been believers and who probably never will be. It's about those of us for whom faith is difficult, but who are trying to work in this direction. One way or another, this story speaks to *all* of us.

It was not enough for his persecutors to put Jesus to death. They had to choose the most painfully cruel and inhumane form of execution they could come up with. But that too wasn't enough. They were determined to humiliate him—hence their insistence that he wear the crown of thorns and carry his own cross up the hill to an execution site that was essentially a garbage dump. But even this wasn't enough, so they crucified him alongside two common thieves. All the while a mob was yelling insults. And to add to his indignity, even one of those two thieves was mocking him. *"If you're so great, how come you're up here with us? If you're really who you say you are, let's see a miracle. Get yourself down from there, and while you're at it, rescue us too."* But suddenly one of these thieves, in a moment of revelation, becomes a believer at nearly the last possible instant. Billy Graham calls this the only deathbed conversion in the whole Bible. This thief then asks Jesus, *"Will you remember me when you get to heaven?"* to which Jesus replies, *"Surely, I say to you, today you will be with me in paradise."*

Clearly, Haydn had his work cut out for him. He faced two challenges. First, to compose music that captures, from the very first note, all the hopelessness, the stress, and the darkness of those desperate moments. Second, to somehow come up with a way to illustrate, through music, the instant conversion of the "good thief." This second goal is achieved through a rather conventional compositional technique that we call *harmonic modulation*. Here is how it works. The movement begins in the key of C minor, which is the traditional "storm and stress" key. (It is no coincidence that *The Earthquake* movement is also in C minor.) From the very first note, we are overwhelmed by the pathos of this dark and desolate music. We eventually come to a *fermata* (a held note) on the *dominant* of C minor, a resting point on a G chord. It's as if we have reached a fork in the road from which we can proceed (harmonically speaking) in any number of different directions. Our instincts tell us that we will continue in C minor after this brief respite. But instead, Haydn raises the music up a third to the key of E-flat major, to what we call the *relative major* of C minor. We then hear the most heavenly music imaginable—the promise of paradise. Though the accompaniment is different, the melody is essentially the same as the one we heard at the very beginning. But what before was utterly hopeless is suddenly filled with promise. What was before shrouded in darkness now has a radiant glow!

TRACK 4

This sonata, like each of the other six, is composed in what is called *binary form*. As this term implies, the movement consists of two parts that are similar in length and general architecture. In fact, we can point to any place in the second half of this movement and find its antecedent in the first half. It therefore should come as no surprise that the second half begins with music of the same dark and hopeless character that we heard at the very beginning of the movement. By a somewhat different route this time, we eventually reach the now-familiar fork in the road: the *dominant* of C, the *fermata* on a G chord. This time, though, we are even more unsure what Haydn has in store for us. The first time we visited this landmark, we expected to continue in C minor with more dark and hopeless music. But he surprised us by raising everything up to the *relative major* for music that conveyed the promise of paradise. What will Haydn do this time?

TRACK 5

C major, the simplest of all possible solutions! This is the key with no adorning sharps or flats, the tonality where every note of the melody and the accompaniment can be played on the piano using only the white keys. What better way could there possibly be to illustrate the clarity and purity of faith—faith made ever more powerful by its utter simplicity.

"Woman, behold your son!"
"Behold your mother!"

At this point Jesus looks down from the Cross and regards his mother and John, his "beloved disciple." He leaves them in each other's care, saying *"Woman, behold your son!" "Behold your mother!"* To all Christians (and to Catholics in particular) these words have profound significance, which extends well beyond these two individuals. By viewing Mary as the mother of all disciples, and John as their representative, Jesus is in effect forging a new community. Beyond these important theological implications, this word also seems to have reminded Haydn of the fundamental concepts of motherhood and womanhood. One of the reasons this word and the very next one resonate so profoundly today—to believers and nonbelievers alike—is because they relate to two recurring themes in our post-Freudian society: the sometimes difficult embrace of the mother, and the abandonment by the father. This helps to explain why this music can be appreciated on various levels.

One of the great twentieth-century composers was Zoltán Kodály, a Hungarian. Because he was also a conductor, a teacher, a musicologist, and an ethnomusicologist, he was as well-rounded a musician as one can imagine. Though he is probably best known as the teacher of Béla Bartók, he made other major contributions to music education. Among these is a system for the teaching of singing and music-reading to young children, which is still very much in use today in many parts of the world. In designing this system, Kodály sought to identify the two musical notes that would be easiest and most natural for children to sing and remember. He chose two notes because with only one, we don't quite yet have music. We have a sound, a noise, a tone, perhaps even a beautiful one. With two notes, though, we have at least the possibility of music since there now exists the potential for interaction between notes. Kodály systematically searched the musical cultures of the world for the two notes most natural for young children, and what he came up with was *sol-mi*: the fifth degree falling to the third degree of our major scale, forming the interval of a minor third.

This is something that sounds very familiar to all of us, as if it has always been in our blood. It is the playground call of virtually all children. More apropos here, these are the two notes with which children call their mothers.[2]

TRACK 6

Not surprisingly, these same two notes are also at the core of that timeless taunt among children.

TRACK 7

There seems to be something universal about these two notes, something that was apparent not only to Zoltán Kodály but also to others, including those born two centuries earlier. For these are the very same two notes that Haydn chose to use as the basis for his musical contemplation of Jesus calling out from the Cross to his mother.

This sonata opens with three E major chords that establish a radiant and loving atmosphere. We then hear the two-note motive, repeated, as is the norm in this piece. What then follows is a lovely, curving line of music that could not possibly be anything but feminine in character. This answering part of the opening phrase seems, both literally and figuratively, to serve as Mary's answer to Jesus' call from the Cross. It lends a heartbreaking tenderness to the entire sonata—a tenderness that prevails even in its darker moments.

TRACK 8

"My God, my God, why have you forsaken me?"

These words represent what Pastor Jeremiah Wright calls "the ultimate abandonment"—the abandonment of Jesus, in his moment of greatest need, by God. To this day, Jesus' piercing, unanswered cries of *"why?"* continue to haunt many of the faithful because (to paraphrase Peter Gomes) either God has abandoned his own son on the Cross, or Jesus doubts that God will come to his aid. Either way, believers have reason to wonder what this means to *them*—to those who have placed their faith in God and Jesus, both of whom now suddenly appear to have lost faith in each other. Andrew Greeley addresses the dilemma even more bluntly: "Either God can help us and doesn't, in which case he is a poor parent and a bad lover. Or he can't help us and he's not God."

Theologians explain that this ultimate abandonment not only *appears* to be real, but *is* real. It *must be* real in order for the Passion itself to be real—not just the heartwarming parts like Jesus forgiving his murderers, extending the promise of paradise to the thief, and expressing his concern for looking after the human family, but *all* of it. If believers are to be convinced of God's love for mankind, if proof of God's love is the sacrifice of his own son for mankind's sake, then this abandonment must be credible. Not only must the faithful believe it, but Jesus had to believe it too as he was hanging there in the eerie darkness of that horror-filled Friday afternoon. That is why his cries were not filled with imaginary, theoretical, or hypothetical anguish. The fear, the doubt, the panic, and every bit of the resulting anguish were all real.

One assumes that Haydn would have no difficulty expressing the emotions that Jesus felt as he was suspended from that wooden stake. The far more daunting challenge is to provide appropriate musical symbolism to illustrate God's abandonment of Jesus.

From the opening phrase, we hear Jesus' desperation as he cries over and over, *"Why have you forsaken me? Why? WHY?"* Meanwhile, we begin to notice that the melody and its accompaniment are often out-of-sync. Now it is our turn to ask, "why?"

The melody's *"why"* note and the accompaniment's late entrance are each time punctuated here by a *forzando,* printed in the music in its abbreviated form: *fz.*

When the melody's *"why"* note enters one beat ahead of the accompaniment, it is temporarily "pulling away," and there is a disquieting tension for that moment just before the harmony "catches up."[3] Music theory teachers call this *anticipation, suspension,* and *resolution.* But here, the sense of "resolution" is repeatedly thwarted when the *"why"* note cries out again and again before the accompaniment has had a chance to realign itself with the melody. This conveys not just a disorienting off-kilter sensation, but a feeling of frustration and even panic, particularly later in the movement when the *"why"* questions ricochet from one instrument to another.

Here they are so compressed that they actually overlap as one voice begins to "ask" the question before the previous voice has had a chance to finish "asking" it. This is sometimes called *stretto,* and these pile-ups fuel the music's frenzy.

I once counted the number of times Haydn repeats this *"why"* question, and found more than two dozen. With all this repetition, one might think the music would become predictable and tedious. But because each of these unanswered *"whys"* is slightly different, the tension actually builds instead of subsides. Sometimes the melody's question is "asked" plaintively, other times angrily and defiantly. It can be a loud wail, or a hushed, halting whisper. Each and every time, we wait for some sort of "answer" in the subsequent music. But each and every time when it *doesn't* come, we are "left hanging." Listen now to a little of the beginning of this movement—the darkest of all the sonatas.

TRACK 9

Finally, about two-thirds of the way through the movement, we hear a couple of grunts from the cello, like careless, offhand shrugs—which *our* cellist plays with consummate indifference. Is this the "response" we have been waiting for? From this point, the first violin's melody begins to twist and turn upon itself, the tension building as it gathers momentum and fervor. As we approach the emotional zenith of the movement—for me, the climax of this entire work—the melody is writhing in agony. But at the very instant we finally reach that climax, we suddenly notice that the other three instruments have stopped playing! Who ever heard of all but one player dropping out at the musical high point of any composition? Shouldn't we expect all sorts of frenzied activity—trills, tremolos, fortissimo forzandos—from every available quadrant? Ah, but think again. Look what Haydn has done. At the moment of *its* greatest need, the melody has literally been abandoned by the accompaniment!

TRACK 10

"I THIRST."

"I thirst" is one of the shortest complete sentences in the English language. It consists of two words. One syllable each. Two syllables altogether. In Greek, the language that most scholars believe the Gospels were originally written, it is a one-word complete sentence: *"Dipho."* Again, two syllables. In Latin, the language that Haydn used in his manuscript, it is also a short, one-word sentence: *"Sitio."* Yet again, two syllables, in Haydn's setting.

Haydn economizes in a similar manner by writing a melody that consists of only two notes. It is as brief as a melody can be. Nevertheless it is a *complete* melody (heard in the first violin part) whose two notes stretch over a relatively long span of time.

Haydn doesn't stop there. He crafts an ingenious pizzicato accompaniment in the second violin and viola parts that again consists of two notes. (Incidentally, these plucking sounds might remind you of droplets of liquid, possibly referring to the sour wine mentioned in John's Gospel.) Though these two notes alternate back and forth and are played four to eight times faster, they are still the very same two notes we hear in the first violin's melody. Let's listen to this pizzicato accompaniment, which provides the foundation for the first violin's two-note melody that rests on top.

TRACK 11

At the very beginning of the movement, before that first phrase is heard, Haydn writes a snappy little introductory flourish—something to get our attention and perhaps to send a signal. This compact little gesture could have consisted of any number of notes. But what do you think he chose? That's right: two notes. Here they are.

TRACK 12

173

Every composition must have a meter, a time signature that is indicated by the numbers at the beginning of the first line of music. In Haydn's day there were fewer than a dozen possibilities. Today we have many more options since music is rhythmically more complicated now than in the late eighteenth century. The most common meter then was 4/4—four beats per measure, with every quarter note receiving a beat. For that reason it was referred to as "common time." Other choices were 2/4, 3/4, 3/8, 6/8, 9/8, and 12/8. What do you think Haydn chose for this movement? 2/2!

Immediately after the two-note introductory gesture, we hear (naturally) two very different characters of music. The first character is obviously an expression of the *literal* meaning of *"I thirst."* Here we can so easily imagine a man who is near death, his strength sapped from him, his throat parched, his tongue like sandpaper, his lips blistering, barely able to choke out the words *"I thirst."* But suddenly in the very next phrase there is music of a shockingly different temperament. We can still clearly identify the two-note *"I thirst"* motive, this time in the viola. But the music is now powerful, filled with strength, vitality, and almost defiant self-righteousness—hardly the sort of thing we would associate with someone in Jesus' weakened condition. How can this be? We suspect a metaphor, but the one that most readily comes to mind—Jesus "thirsting" for God—does not fit the music at all. So we have to look deeper. Think about that as we listen to the entire opening of this sonata.

TRACK 13

By now we realize that unless we are going to be content with a shallow appreciation of the music, it is necessary to have more than a superficial understanding of the scripture upon which it is based. Yes, there *is* a metaphor here, but it's a very complicated metaphor, one that even world-class scholars can have difficulty explaining with precision and clarity. So perhaps the best way for me, a musician, to convey the meaning of this metaphor, the metaphor that Haydn expresses musically, is to have you imagine a righteously loving father who says to *his* children (with a love that burns passionately and defiantly), *"I THIRST! I THIRST so that your lives might be quenched!"* The music's second character finally makes sense.

Take a step back. Observe what Haydn has accomplished within the first minute of this movement. First, he has conveyed the *literal* meaning of the words that are the inspiration for the sonata. Then he has expressed them as a complex *metaphor.* I challenge you to come up with even one other example in the history of music where a composer has been able to do *that* so effectively!

We're awed.

"IT IS FINISHED!"

Since Jesus says these words during the bleakest moments of his life, some might interpret them as a confession of concession. Far from it! This is an expression of triumphant satisfaction from someone who has successfully completed what he had started. Having "come full circle," he is finally able to view at the end what he had set out to do at the beginning. The beginning and the end are thus reunited and reconciled, and from this point new beginnings are now possible.

As difficult as it is to explain this concept in words, it is even more challenging to convey it through music. But this is precisely what Haydn does in this movement. At the outset, the sonata's five-note "motto" is displayed: G, E-flat, C, D, and G—the 1st, 6th, 4th, 5th, and (again) the 1st degree of the scale.

TRACK 14

These notes correspond to the five Latin syllables *"con-sum-ma-tum est"*— which, as previously mentioned, was Haydn's own musical autograph that he often wrote at the bottom of a page of music or correspondence. (See this book's final page.) Perhaps the most obvious feature of these five notes is that they too "come full circle" in that they begin and end on the same pitch.

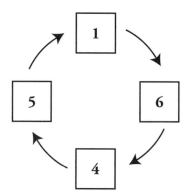

Moreover, their order suggests an interesting symmetry. Note "1" is on both ends of this row of notes. In between are the remaining notes: "6," "4," and "5." The middle note, "4," is preceded and followed by two notes (6 and 1 and 5 and 1), which approach it from above.

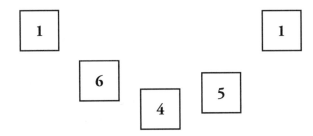

Just as Haydn crafted both a melody and an accompaniment from the same two notes in *"I thirst,"* he uses this group of five notes as the prototype for both the melody and the harmony throughout this movement. In *solfeggio* (where Italian syllables correspond to the notes) they form the following melody: *do, la, fa, sol, do.* However, they are also the bass notes of the following harmonic progression: I, VI, IV, V, I. This, of course, is one of the most common chord sequences in all music—so common, so basic, that it is probably the first set of chords learned by every starry-eyed teenager who plays guitar in his own garage band. Haydn's "common touch" is thus evident here. The choice of these particular chords as the foundation upon which everything else in the movement is built suggests that the music's underlying message is one that can underscore the lives of every one of *us*, one way or another. Not only is there an inherent symmetry in the music, there is also an inherent unity because of the interdependence of the melody and the harmony. This, then, symbolizes the symmetry and unity of the concept of "coming full circle," which is the essence of *"It is finished!"*

It is significant that this is one of only two movements (out of nine) that begins in one mode (minor) but ends in the other (major).[4] Neither an accident nor a coincidence, this is an ingenious way for Haydn to demonstrate through his music the reconciliation of "the beginning" and "the end"—through the reconciliation of G minor and G major. Listen now to a little more of the beginning of this movement.

TRACK 15

As the music washes over us, we may not always be aware of all the sophisticated ways Haydn uses the five-note motto as the basis for this movement's architecture. But neither are we always conscious of the inherent unity and symmetry of other things around us—in the "architecture" of a flower, for instance, or the precise patterns that were so meticulously calculated by M. C. Escher in his mesmerizing "metamorphosis" drawings. Nevertheless, the inherent unity that we sense in all these examples— and particularly in this sonata by Haydn—instills in us a feeling of stability and assurance that is a consequence of combining something that has extraordinary sensory appeal with an orderly organization of form and function. We may experience this only on a subconscious level, but we "feel" it nonetheless. It is as if everything in this movement has been worked out in advance so that somehow things can "work out" for us in the end.

When hearing this sonata for the first time, even some listeners who are *not* expecting a bleak confession of concession are surprised by the effortless, lighthearted, and almost casual character of much of the music. In trying to match the tone of this music to the deeper significance of the text upon which it was based, Haydn was searching for ways to *lift* the burden, *release* the tension, allow the music to "breathe" more freely, and even let it begin to "dance." How ironic: crucifixion, which causes death by asphyxiation, is portrayed by music that "breathes!" How inconsistent with the narrow logic of our preconceptions: crucifixion music that "dances!" With this musical "ending," then, we can look back with a sense of fulfillment at what was accomplished, while also looking ahead to the possibilities of new "beginnings." Once we have reached that point, once we understand why this music *must* "breathe" and "dance," *we* will have "come full circle."

"FATHER, INTO YOUR HANDS
I COMMEND MY SPIRIT."

Since this was the final utterance of a man who would die moments later, one might predict that Haydn would choose music that is frail, vulnerable, and almost lifeless. But what we hear instead has surprising vitality, strength, assurance, and resolve. That is because these words express the conviction that resonates within every faithful believer: that if you put your trust in God, you will be all right, no matter what happens. Listen now to the opening of this sonata, to music that so perfectly captures that feeling of confidence and loving trust that is inherent in Jesus' final statement.

TRACK 16

Haydn has often used symbolism in this work, and some of it is rather complex. But here we are at death's door, where, as Peter Gomes has reminded us, things tend to be pretty simple, pretty basic, pretty uncomplicated. It makes sense, then, for Haydn to choose symbolism that is disarmingly simple. At the very end of the movement we hear the two violins, quietly moving together. They are separated sometimes by the interval of a third, a fifth, or a sixth. When one violin takes a step, the other takes a similar step, and they are never separated by more than a few steps. The meaning is clear. If you entrust your life and spirit to God, you are never alone because God takes every step with you. He is sometimes very near, sometimes not. But He is always present. On our original CD—in some of the most powerfully moving preaching you are ever likely to hear—Rev. Martin Luther King Jr. puts it this way: "You know that God walks with you. Even though you walk through the valley of the shadow of death, you know that God is there. Even though you stand amid the giant shadow of disappointment, you don't despair, because you know God is with you."

Listen now to this movement's conclusion. No longer is there any hint of fear or doubt. Eternity holds its breath as we await whatever is to follow with quiet and trusting confidence.

TRACK 17

THE EARTHQUAKE

Notice how quietly, how peacefully the previous movement ends. There is not quite a sense of timelessness, however, since the music's barely audible pulse is still regularly beating. Some may imagine this to be Jesus' pulse, gradually fading to almost nothing, finally stopping altogether. For others it is a reminder that a master clock is still ticking, that time is quietly marching toward an inevitable conclusion. In either case the music, now utterly weightless, seems to evaporate, to gently and slowly rise in a heavenward direction.

Besides painting a breathtakingly poignant sound-picture, this extended and suspended *diminuendo* also helps Haydn solve the next movement's biggest technical problem: how in the world to make a mere string quartet sound like an earthquake! By ending this previous movement *pianissimo, sempre piu piano*, Haydn coaxes our ears to listen with hypersensitivity to every real and imagined sound. He also does something else that is radical and unique: he specifies that the entire movement should be played with mutes, *con sordini*—the only time he does this in his eighty-plus string quartets.[5] All of this enables the very next sounds we hear, the first *fortissimo* notes of *The Earthquake*, to seem even louder than they really are. Another shocker is the tempo. Marked *presto*, this is the only fast movement in the entire piece, thus interrupting the steady pace and predictable flow of the eight previous *adagios*. Haydn's instructions that the entire finale must be played *con tutta la forza* take on even greater significance when we recognize that nowhere else in his other string quartets does he demand louder and more aggressive sounds from the players.

But even this is not quite enough to reproduce the terrifying cacophonous din of the rumbling and sundering earth as it quakes uncontrollably underfoot. So Haydn virtually abandons the *homophonic texture*—the melody and accompaniment style—that he has used not only in every other movement of this work, but also in most movements of his other string quartets. In this final movement the melody is almost never played by one instrument alone, but is played by either all four at once, *tutti*, or by pairs of instruments. Even Haydn's pairings are clever. It is always the top half (the two violins) versus the bottom half (the viola and cello). As these two mighty duos alternate, ripping into sharp, *staccato,* jagged, *forzando* musical fragments, listeners have the impression of being in the middle of a cataclysm, of chunks of earth and shards of rock flying at them from both sides. The earthquake's massive tremors, produced by huge *tremolando* effects, never subside but suddenly cease at the very end of the piece. Listen now to a portion of this stunning *finale.*

TRACK 18

THE HISTORY OF MEDITATION ON JESUS' SEVEN LAST WORDS

GROVER A. ZINN

The book that you have taken up to read is much like a mosaic. Or perhaps I should say that it is a mosaic in the process of formation and final completion—a process that requires the participation of you, the reader. Mosaics, of course, are made up of small pieces of colored glass or other material, placed together in a pattern to form figures such as a face, an animal, a vase, or an abstract design. One can liken the meditations enclosed between the covers of this book to those small colored pieces, called *tesserae*, which make up the figures in a mosaic. Each piece shares a specific color with some of the other pieces in the mosaic. At the same time, each piece also has its own individual shape: some are square, some rectangular, some irregular; some are perfectly flat, others have a surface curved "in" or "out" or textured in some way. So it is with these meditations. They come in seven basic "colors," as it were, for each is directly and deeply attached to one of the Seven Last Words of Christ. But each meditation also has a distinctive shape and a texture that result from the creative work of the author of that meditation as she or he shaped words and ideas to convey a message, a meaning, drawn from one of the last phrases uttered by Jesus as He hung dying on the Cross.

The individual pieces, the *tesserae*, have a place in relation to the other *tesserae* that compose a mosaic, and the result is a pattern in which the meaning of the whole far transcends that of the individual parts. This creation of larger relationships and patterns is what the editor and the writers/speakers hope will result from your reading of this book. First, there will no doubt be an appreciation of the individual "pieces," the meditations themselves. Then will come a pattern developed by you, the attentive reader, as you devise a use for these meditations that relates their meaning to your life in some specific way. The mosaic may change from day to day or month to month. It may have only one form from the beginning. It may be the case that you read this book through once from cover to cover, put it on the shelf, and take it down on various occasions. On the other hand, you may find yourself selecting one meditation at a time from each "word" and thus reading your gathering of "pieces" in a pattern of your own making and meaning. Then again, another reader may find a word or phrase in a single meditation that provides the starting point for his or her own continuing reflection on some theme, much like an Episcopal priest who once told me that when he was an auditor, not a celebrator, of the Eucharist, he often found a single word or phrase in the prayers that sparked his meditative reflection.

The rhythm of reading has many variations, many possibilities, many opportunities for expression and impression. The possibilities are, in one sense, endless. These meditations plumb the depths of life at the point of death, the meaning of love in the midst of cruel torture, the creation of new relations while enduring piercing pain. Yet the possibilities are, in another way, limited. But they are limited in a way that encourages creativity, in the same way that the closely defined form of Japanese haiku evokes both terseness in composition and a depth beyond imagination. These meditations are tethered to a center around which the pieces revolve and take their places. This center, this point of reference, is a specific life lived out within the Jewish religious culture in the Roman province of Palestine some two thousand years ago. Jesus' life, His death, and His resurrection have since taken on meanings from the experiences of His immediate disciples, from the writings that now make up the Gospels and other parts of the Christian Bible, and from the experiences of Christians over the past two millennia. Our task—the task of those who have written and the task of those who now read—is to allow the great and intense themes of life and death to interweave themselves with two very different "times." First of all, there is the time and place of Jesus' death long ago. This past time, made present in our imaginative "re-presentation," was, as the English hymn-writer Isaac Watts put it, a moment when "sorrow and love flow mingled down" in the draining of Jesus' life-blood from his body.[1] Second, there is the "modern" age in which we live—the times, good and bad, hopeful and fearful, tragic or joyful, in which we find ourselves now measuring out our lives and also taking measure of the lives we live. Not all readers will be followers of the way of Jesus and his disciples, ancient or modern. But no doubt each reader will draw from the same fabric of life's challenging, wearying, and even triumphant moments to make her or his connection with these gathered meditations and the three hours of agony and spiritual insight that form their inspiration.

The mosaic we make of this book is connected with great themes and with moments from the past and present. It is also intimately bound up with magnificent and moving music and with the history of Christian worship. Indeed, the conception of *The Seven Last Words of Christ* is itself a mosaic, so perhaps a few words on that part of our mosaic will be appropriate before moving to the music and then to Christian worship, past and present.

Any attentive reader of the four Gospels soon becomes aware that the Gospels differ in points minor and major as they recount Jesus' last days and hours. Matthew and Mark have only one "word" from the lips of the dying Jesus, the awful and awesome cry of dereliction: *"Eli, Eli, lama sabachtani? My God, my God, why have you forsaken me?"* In this, Jesus repeats the Psalmist's agonized cry of distress and desertion by the Holy One (Psalm 22:1; Vulgate 21:1). In the traditional numbering of the "words," this is the fourth and central word. The Gospel of Luke has three "words" and omits the one recounted by Mark and Matthew. Luke has the first "word": *"Father, forgive them, for they know not what they do";* the second: *"Surely, I say to you, today you will be with me in paradise";* and the seventh: *"Father, into your hands I commend my spirit."*

The Gospel of John has a different set of three "words." They are the third, fifth, and sixth in the ordered series of utterances: *"Woman, behold your son!" "Behold your mother!"; "I thirst"*; and *"It is finished!"*

The prism of each Gospel refracts a different spectrum of light from the last hours of Jesus' life. For Mark and Matthew, the great cry of desolation dominates the narrative and casts a monochromatic light upon the scene. The Gospel of Luke has light shot through with multiple hues of forgiveness, deliverance of the outsider, and confidence in the love and healing power of the One whom Jesus called "Father." The light that the Gospel of John sheds upon this landscape of blood and agony reflects yet other aspects. For in John's three "words," Jesus offers the only self-referential words, *"I thirst,"* that escape from his lips during the three hours upon the Cross. He then turns to Mary and John at the foot of the Cross, offering a new triangulation of the loving bond involving mother, son, and friend. Finally, the gasping cry *"It is finished!"* declares the end at hand.

It is probable that *"Woman, behold your son!" "Behold your mother!"* has been the direct inspiration of more depictions of the crucifixion than any other source. Thousands of images from the Middle Ages onward show Christ hanging upon the wood of the Cross with a grieving Mary standing on Christ's right and the Evangelist John on Christ's left, in poignant representation of this "third word." In Europe and England by about 1050–1060 C.E., manuscript paintings of this scene were to be found in Psalters and other books.[2] As the decades passed, the popularity of this representation of the crucifixion increased, and it could be found in panel paintings, ivory carvings, sculpted church façades, and the like. The later Middle Ages came to favor a more dramatic and all-encompassing rendering of the entire scene with soldiers, the crowd, the two "thieves," and many other details.

In 1786 Haydn accepted a commission from the canons of the Cathedral of Cadiz in Spain to compose music for a three-hour Good Friday service based on the seven last words of Christ with meditations on each to be delivered by the bishop. Immediately he realized the demands that the occasion placed upon him. Richard Young has much to say about Haydn and the music elsewhere in this book. I want to add a few remarks on the words, the music, and the particular form the service took. On the one hand, Haydn expressed the desire to create music of such transparent meaning that any person who heard it would understand the music and its intent, namely, to represent the seven last words of Christ. Listening to the seven *adagios,* so profound in their simplicity and simple in their profundity, confirms that Haydn succeeded. But he also had another musical desire in mind: to represent the actual words themselves. Haydn not only wrote the Latin text of the relevant "word" above the opening of each *adagio*. Evidence from contemporaries suggests that he also consciously structured each opening phrase according to the rhythm of the "word" being represented. Thus, by means of the opening measures, and with rhythmic, harmonic, and/or melodic patterns recurring throughout each *adagio*, the attentive listener is "reminded" of the words that lie behind or, perhaps better said, lie within Haydn's music. The power of such composition is one of the things that leads to the universality and the emotive power of this music for the Seven Last Words.

The type of service for which Haydn composed this music is both very "old" and relatively "new" in terms of forms of Good Friday worship. It was "old" according to what we know of Holy Week services in Jerusalem in the late fourth century C.E. It was "new" in terms of *when* the type of service Haydn describes is first found in the early-modern church.

A fourth-century pilgrim to Jerusalem, Egeria, gave a detailed account of Jerusalem Holy Week services in a letter to her friends living somewhere in Spain (or perhaps Gaul).[3] Her description shows that much of the subsequent Holy Week liturgy of the Western (Roman Catholic) Church was indebted to rituals developed in Jerusalem for pilgrims to the holy sites of the last week of Jesus' life. Two services at the Church of the Holy Sepulcher, built by the Emperor Constantine (dedicated ca. 335), are especially notable. Egeria describes a three-hour service on Good Friday that lasted from noon until 3 P.M. During the service, numerous biblical texts (from the Gospels, Epistles, and Jewish prophets) related to the crucifixion were read, while the congregation of pilgrims and others wept and lamented. This is the "old" connection for the three hours' service at Cadiz. It was thoroughly displaced in medieval and modern times by another devotion also celebrated on

Good Friday in Jerusalem at the Church of the Holy Sepulcher. (The "new" connection for the Cadiz service is the "modern" three hours' service described below.) The fourth-century ceremony destined to survive in continuity in Christian ritual was the "Adoration of the Cross"—that is, venerating and kissing the reliquary containing the pieces of the True Cross discovered in Jerusalem ca. 326 C.E. by Helena, mother of the Emperor Constantine. Pilgrims and others gathered at the church on Good Friday morning. The bishop and clergy displayed the relics of the Cross so that the laity might approach and venerate ("adore") them. The devotion and service spread, first to churches that were fortunate enough to have a fragment of the Cross (many did) and then to churches that displayed merely a cross or crucifix for the faithful to venerate in the service.

The Good Friday observance of the "liturgical churches" (e.g., Roman Catholic and Anglican) came to have three parts:[4]

1. The reading of the Passion according to the Gospel of John and other scripture (the "three lessons") and a series of solemn prayers;
2. The ancient ceremony of the Adoration of the Cross (called in the Middle Ages "Creeping to the Cross" because of the prostration of clergy and devotees before the cross on the altar);
3. Mass celebrated with a Host consecrated on the previous day (Mass of the Presanctified).

In the Middle Ages (and in some cases later) this threefold service was often followed by a dramatic "entombment" of a consecrated Eucharistic host (the Body of Christ) in a specially constructed "sepulcher" in a side chapel, with the subsequent "resurrection" of the Host on Easter morning.[5] Where practiced, this was a moving reenactment of the burial and resurrection of Jesus.

The emergence of a "modern" service called the "three hours' service" focused on the Seven Last Words of Christ—the "new" connection of the Cadiz ceremony referred to above—goes back to a provincial city on the edge of an empire, during a time of public crisis in the early modern period. Scholars agree that the first "three hours' service"—with the reading of each "word" from the Cross, followed by a meditation and accompanied by hymns, chants, and private meditation—took place in the seventeenth century in Peru under Spanish domination. Precise dating is uncertain, but a Jesuit priest, Alonso Messia (1665–1732), of great influence among the local population, seems to have instituted a three hours' devotion as the result of a series of earthquakes that shook the area in 1687.[6] From later published pamphlets that insist upon the original form of the service (apparently as the devotion spread, local variations quickly sprang up), Father Messia's innovative devotional service was comprised of an introductory exhortation by the Jesuit, followed by the reading of the first "word" and a homily/meditation, with the congregation then joining in various canticles and hymns, concluding with the recitation of the *Pater Noster* and *Ave Maria*. The pattern was then repeated for each successive "word." The service was so timed that with the recitation of the Creed at the end of the service, the phrase *crucifixus et mortuus est* was said as the bell tolled 3 P.M. The pamphlets commending the "proper" form of the three hours' devotion according to the founder's plan also contain his meditation on each word.

This particular devotional exercise seems to have spread fairly quickly throughout Jesuit missions in the Americas and then to Italy, especially to the Gesú, the main Jesuit church in Rome. In 1789 Pope Pius VI granted a plenary indulgence in connection with the service at the Gesú. The service spread to Spain in the eighteenth century as well. By the early nineteenth century, English Jesuits were celebrating it in their churches. One may suspect that similar Good Friday services, developed by the Oratorians in Rome and later at the Brompton Oratory in London, supported the swelling popularity of this kind of service. Although the enthusiasm for the "three hours' service" that evoked Haydn's seven *adagios* on Christ's last words belongs to Catholicism, this pattern of devotion leapt from Catholic to Protestant congregations in nineteenth-century England and continues to flourish and spread in both Catholic and Protestant venues today.

It is perhaps an irony of history that a service that has become so central in the Holy Week devotions of millions of Christians in Europe and the Americas should have been "invented" by a Jesuit priest in the late seventeenth century, in an area of the Americas colonized by Spain. Equally intriguing is the leap from Catholic to Protestant churches in nineteenth-century England. Without recounting the dizzying fluctuations of ritual observance in nineteenth-century Anglicanism, it is enough to recall that the so-called ritualists, who were intent on introducing traditional and ancient (to opponents, "Roman and Popish") liturgical practices were responsible for the first celebrations of the "three hours' service." Rev. Alexander H. Mackonochie, a member of the Anglo-Catholic wing of the Church of England, is reputedly the first Anglican priest to celebrate the Three Hours' Service.[7] This he did in the early 1860s in his parish of St. Albans, Holborn, London, before he was driven from that parish by church officials opposed to his radical (he would have said, "traditional") liturgical innovations. By 1864 the service had been celebrated in Manchester, England. In 1879, St. Paul's Cathedral in London held its first Three Hours' Service. A published set of "Addresses in the form of meditations" by W. J. Knox-Little, entitled *The Three Hours' Agony of Our Blessed Redeemer,* gives insight into the spirit of the new Anglican service. Knox-Little delivered these addresses at St. Alban's Church, Manchester, on Good Friday of 1877.[8] In his introduction he urges that his congregation think of the Passion as a great drama and strive to bridge two chasms: time and space, as they journey mentally to Calvary and Jesus' Cross. Knox-Little's evocation of time, place, and emotional response stands in the tradition of Messia and his Jesuit confreres, who were masters (via the *Spiritual Exercises* of Ignatius Loyola) of developing an inner visualization of sacred scenes. Jesus' words are seen by Knox-Little as probing the great themes of life and death, love and duty, a mother's agony and a son's benevolence.

Precisely how the devotion came to North America is not clear. One noted scholar of Catholic worship has commented that the history of the Three Hours' Service has never been adequately studied.[9] A well-known American Protestant liturgiologist touches on the Three Hours' Service with the brief remark that it is "a seventeenth-century Hispanic rite from Peru."[10] The current state of the Three Hours' Service is illuminating, however. It is acknowledged to be the dominant form of Good Friday observance, even among Anglicans (Episcopalians in the United States) and Catholics, whose liturgies retain the Adoration of the Cross as the proper liturgical service. Interestingly, the Methodist *Book of Worship* adopted by the General Conference of 1964 presented two services for Good Friday: a Three Hours' Service for the afternoon and a Good Friday evening service that includes the "Adoration at the Cross" (the Gospel, Deprecations, and Adoration of the Cross) but omits a communion service, which would be the Methodist equivalent of the Mass of the Presanctified.[11] Methodists were honoring the "old" and the "new" as they revised their 1944 *Book of Worship*. An African-American church in Brooklyn holds a yearly ecumenical Three Hours' Service; a small Episcopalian parish in an Ohio village does the same. Such is the nature of the Three Hours' Service that a historian of American religion has observed to me that it is possibly the most ecumenical moment in the church year.

A brief "surf" of the Internet (appropriate for this electronically linked age) suggests the contemporary variety in settings for the three hours' service. In Columbus, Ohio, on Good Friday 2003, Trinity Episcopal Church celebrated the Stations of the Cross (a devotional practice popularized by Franciscans in the later Middle Ages) in a very public way around Capitol Square, and then held a Three Hours' Service with preachers invited from various "walks" of Episcopalian life. In a somewhat different vein, the parish church of St. Lawrence, Chobham, in Surrey, England, celebrated the Three Hours' Service with the rector's meditations "looking at some familiar fairy stories." In Ireland the former Bishop of Connor (preaching in Co. Armagh in September 2000) recalled not only the horror of "Bloody Friday" but also the need for forgiveness, sorrow, and reconciliation. He went on to mention moments of kindness extended to and from Catholic parishes and their Church of Ireland (Anglican) counterparts. Especially noteworthy for the bishop was a "Procession of Witness" in Connor, on Good Friday, from the Catholic Cathedral of St. Peter to the Church of Ireland Cathedral of St. Anne's, with the procession arriving for the Three Hours' Service at St. Anne's. What better work for a Three Hours' Service than such reconciliation? As a final evocation of ecumenical gatherings, I note the worship schedule for Lent and Holy Week in Droitwich Spa (Worchestershire, England): Lent saw meetings in the Anglican, Baptist, Roman Catholic, Methodist, Emmanuel AOG, and Salvation Army churches, with Palm Sunday services at Anglican and Roman Catholic venues, Maundy Thursday at the

Salvation Army, and on Good Friday, the Ecumenical Walk of Witness from Sacred Heart (Roman Catholic) Church to the Anglican Church (St. Andrew's), which held the Three Hour's Service and an accompanying "Children's Workshop." It was obviously a busy Lenten season, weaving the ecumenical fabric and constructing the ecumenical mosaic in Droitwich Spa.

The pieces of the mosaic lie before you, reader. There are meditations to be read; there is Haydn's music to be heard; there are words to savor, words to probe, and words that will probe you. What you make of this collection lies in your power. The speakers/authors have finished their words; the players have played their music, and some of them have also spoken/written their words. This little craft is now launched upon the sea of the world. May it find a safe haven in your mind, through your eyes, ears, and heart.

CHRIST'S FINAL UTTERANCES IN TODAY'S WORLD

JEAN BETHKE ELSHTAIN

There are philosophers and linguists who insist that a word means what it means, no more and no less. They go on to argue that a word designates or stipulates: I point, utter a word that designates the thing pointed to, and that is the end of the matter. Beyond the circle of such rigid stalwarts, however, a word—not just any word—may shimmer with possibility. A word—not just any word—may draw us into a dark and lonely place and leave us haunted. A word—not just any word— may slam us back against our seats with such force that we feel as if we have been slapped. A word—not just any word—may tickle out a smile, perhaps induce a belly-laugh. A word—not just any word—may bring hope to the hopeless, cheer to the cheerless, and a glimmer of recognition to one who, up to a given moment, never had a clue.

There are words that seem to be living things. In a very real sense they are. Such words come to us heavy, not light. They are the decoctions of centuries of wisdom, fear, loneliness, betrayal, love, elation, and recognition. Surely the seven last words of Jesus the Christ belong in such company. Burnished over the centuries, such words are a palpable presence. No empty vessel or box into which we pour meaning willy-nilly, these words provoke, challenge, and humble us. Christ's final utterances have been spoken so often since that dreadful day on Calvary, and their meaning has been refracted over the centuries in so many contexts, that we quail at the prospect of offering something new, fresh, wise, on our own, so that we might add our own slight contribution to that mound of compressed human meaning. Such words we approach with fear and trembling. What more can we, can I, possibly say?

As one who studies human political life and the ethics that undergirds and animates such life, I am struck by the ways in which cultures may gain brave and wonderful new words—"all men are created equal"—and then watch as those words take flight, take on a life of their own, and bring to bear over time outcomes the authors of those words would no doubt have found astounding. Though, again, maybe not in the case of the American Declaration of Independence. Jefferson himself understood that slavery could not survive indefinitely in a nation based on such words, and Lincoln saw to it that this was the case. Potent words enter a culture's bloodstream and then make their way through it again and again, picking up fresh oxygen and no doubt much in the way of grit and even contaminants along the way. This is no pristine process. We add and subtract as we go and, in the case of good and powerful words, we hope that there will be many more additions than there are subtractions.

Let me illustrate what I have in mind. In a seminar a few years back I required the students to read British author P. D. James's *Children of Men,* a novel of a terrible future world in which no children have been born on planet earth for several decades. Then, a miraculous pregnancy. A rush to find safety by the pregnant mother and her small family, an entourage that includes a midwife rescuer of the baby. This woman's name is Miriam. I looked up from the text and said something along these lines, "Of course, you will pick up the reference—the name 'Miriam'—so let's talk about the significance of James's choice of this name for the female rescuer of this 'miracle baby.'" To my astonishment, not a single graduate student in the room that day knew the significance of the name "Miriam." Musing on that experience, I realized how worlds can be lost and words can lose meaning. Our Bible-shaped world is one that is gradually losing much of its resonance for much of our population. The reference points have gone missing for millions.

I ponder the loss. It isn't just a loss of something as insignificant in the overall scheme of things as not being able to identify the name of Miriam, the sister of Moses, who offers to tend the baby found floating downriver in a basket that is recovered by the Egyptian pharaoh's sister. Think of the thick, dense history and layers of meaning lost if the genealogy of Martin Luther King Jr.'s great "I Have a Dream" speech in the Prophet Amos—and hence the entire prophetic tradition—is just not there. Think of what is lost if the biblical cadences of Lincoln's great Second Inaugural Address go unremarked upon and unappreciated. It isn't the case that all meaning is lost, of course, but critical reference points are, and with the loss of such reference points goes our ability to locate ourselves within complex traditions. We always sit uneasily in traditions, of course. But how on earth can we possibly understand what we are for and against if we have no sense at all of where we have come from, of who has gone before, of what others have said about what we are now pondering?

Christ's final utterances come to us trailing the tears, joys, and beliefs of centuries. I approach the task of writing my commentary on these words for appearances with the Vermeer String Quartet as it performs so beautifully Haydn's great work, with a kind of reverence. I hope to add something but not to detract from what has gone before. I cannot believe that anyone has ever approached these words carelessly, flippantly, or frivolously. I have a hunch that the militant unbeliever and the determined mocker would not agree to be part of an event that, through music and language, aims to help the listener to re-experience, in a mediated but powerful way, those agonizing moments, that most momentous of endings that signaled a beginning that transformed the world.

We are struck by the fact that something ancient—a shard, a fragile piece of parchment, a decaying shroud, a splintered cross—all the artifacts of grief, death, and remembrance are here tapped. But grasp hold of one of those artifacts and you are yanked through time into the present. There is so much that resonates. The air buzzes with possibilities and reference points. *"Father, forgive them, for they know not what they do."* What does that mean in this world? Does it mean the law no longer applies? Has justice been suspended altogether in favor of mercy? God the Father through the Son guarantees with these words that such questions can never be evaded.

"Today you will be with me in paradise." A contrite thief. A dying man's promise. We reflect on desert—what we have earned, what has simply come to us as a gift, beginning with life itself. Can anything possibly be this simple? we wonder. Perhaps grace is a moment of the most extraordinary simplicity. Why, then, is it so hard to believe? Even to accept? Living as we do in an era in which the window to transcendence is slammed shut (in philosopher Charles Taylor's powerful imagery), we find it hard to believe that death could be an entry into anything beyond the grave or the crematorium. But today—He said today. One has the overwhelming sense that to turn this into "mere metaphor" is to do violence to the words.

"Woman, behold your son!" "Behold your mother!" This one aims straight for the gut. A son dying an excruciating death in full view of his mother. Even television sensationalism cannot altogether cheapen this. So many mothers. So many deaths. Pondering these words, all the recent examples come to mind, as does the apparent inability of the world to respond to such deaths in an effective and forthright way. When the world responds with force to interdict massive and planned killings, other ethical quandaries come into play. Nothing simple here. But the potent distillation haunts. In a world of mass death, the biblical text brings it back to where it belongs: *this* mother, *this* son, but the son is gesturing, not to himself, but to another. You, mother, must now regard him as son and he as your mother. There is a dimension to this that hits us as emotionally terrible and healing, at one and the same time. More complexity again.

"My God, my God, why have you forsaken me?" "If God forsaked His only begotten Son, what chance have I got?" might be our immediate, unthinking—but not improbable—reply. These are some of the last words, but they are not the *final* words. For we know the story. This moment of forsakenness is real, and we must drink the forlornness to

196

the last dregs. At some moment or another, we all experience abandonment. Those who cannot get past the moment of abandonment—who
are glued to the spot—may, in their anguish, take their own lives or lash
out and take the lives of others. But we know that the anguish of abandonment here is not in vain; that the suffering is for all of humanity's
sake. We are not God, of course. We cannot suffer for all humanity. But
we can find, out of the cry of anguish, the wisdom that might be ours
through the grace of God.

"I thirst." Straightforward? We know better. There is a direct physical
need. The dying man is parched. Our thirsts are so various and so exi-
gent. Perhaps we no longer recognize the difference between cold, clear
water and poisons. We thirst for so much. Our culture urges us on.
Where there is a lot, we want more. We want to "drink it all in." Our
eyes glimmer with the possibility of all there is to consume. We recall
that the Bible story tells us that some among the crowd mocked the
dying Jesus as he thirsted and received a bit of sour wine from a sponge.
How are we to understand such a moment? Perhaps by considering our
own thirsts and how others respond to them. The counterfeit thirsts are
easily sated—there is always plenty out there. But what of the deeper
thirsts that we find difficult to name? I thirst, but for what?

"It is finished!" It is complete. All that was necessary has come to pass.
How difficult this is for us. Most of us fear that we will leave this life
with our "To Do" list crowded with undone tasks. We will take our final
breaths with a nagging voice in our ears—our own—chiding us for not
having run fast enough, or far enough, or aggressively enough. If there
is an embedded ethic here it is one that calls us to examine our lives in
light of eternity—or some moment other than or beyond the one
in which we presently find ourselves—in order that we might find a
moment of roundedness and completion. Perhaps the much underrated
virtue of endurance comes to mind—our ability to take what comes our
way, to make the best of it, to deal with what has been dealt, to recognize that we are never masters in our own house. Perhaps we are called
to be a bit kinder with ourselves and to understand that completion can
never mean perfection.

The last utterance is one of hope: *"Father, into your hands I commend my spirit."* The moment of abandonment has passed. What is left is a relinquishment—into *your* hands—tethered to the assurance that as we reach out, we will be embraced and accepted. This moment of hope reminds at least some of us of moments of political hope on our troubled globe. Of the extraordinary year 1989 when the sacrifice and hopefulness of brave dissidents in Eastern Europe over a half-century bore fruit as freedom supplanted tyranny. Of marchers singing, "We shall overcome." It is a quiet moment in this final utterance. A moment of understated assurance. There is no such assurance that awaits peoples fighting for human dignity. They may or may not prevail. But what they have won through the struggle itself—through the hopefulness that animates the struggle—is their human dignity. For they have understood something about the human person, namely, that we are creatures, embodied, of this earth but we are also borne beyond.

There are moral philosophers who believe we can capture and summarize the moral life in rather the way some of the language philosophers believe we can pin down words. There are lists of *do's* and *don't's*, each calibrated under the framework of a simple moral code and arrayed around a single overarching human good: justice or utility or some such. The last utterances of Jesus the Christ tell us a very, very different story about the moral life. They are words of life and death, rich, evocative, embrocated with potent emotion. They are words that invite various responses, that perplex us and call us out, and that force us inward to examine our own wellsprings of meaning and purpose. The moral life, they tell us, is not a checklist but a way of being in the world with and among others in all of life's griefs and joys, including its final moments. God please, none among us will be compelled to live through the brutality and anguish of Christ's final moments. But we can pray that we will always remember His final utterances and, on our own life's journey, recall, reflect, and renew our pilgrimage as we do.

LOOKING BACK,
SUMMING UP

Martin E. Marty

Seven "words from the Cross," each with brief commentaries by ten to thirteen respondents in this book, means that by now those who have read all that precedes this postlude have had more than seventy opportunities to reflect on the crucial themes.

When I first heard that these comments were to be published, I pondered the question: Would they hold reader interest? To hear seven different speakers on seven different words at a single performance is one thing. The prospect of collecting seven sets of at least ten texts and presenting them together at book length to readers struck me, at least temporarily, as a repetitious venture that risked inducing boredom.

Now I am ready to say about the product you have just read: No risk. No repetition. No boredom. Readers can test this for themselves. Some may have read all the homilies on "The First Word" in sequence, then on another occasion all the pages about "The Second Word," and so on. Others may have chosen to assemble their own packages, reading seven commentaries per sitting, one for each word. It is likely in either case that they, and you, encountered fresh angles of vision and surprising motifs, the collection of which served to inspire imaginations.

Listeners to music who enjoy pieces called "theme and variations" never need tire, thanks to the changes of rhythm, harmony, melody, tempo, and expression from one variation to the next. Viewers of photography exhibits appreciate the chance to see what different lighting and various perspectives do to a single subject. Monet has enthralled countless gallery-goers who view his paintings of the haystacks or water-lily ponds mounted in a row, each of them revealing something different. No risk. No repetition. No boredom.

The appended biographies of the speakers suggest in part why their perspectives differ so much. Read or reread the short biographies and connect them with the essays. The project will be revealing, since the biographies usually evoke something of the communities of faith or the vocation, ethnicity, or personal experiences of each speaker, and these color what they have to say.

The Vermeer Quartet conceives of *The Seven Last Words of Christ* and the incident that inspired it as something around which they had no right to install fences or build walls. In the "you-all-come" spirit with which the figure of Jesus in the Gospels is always identified, they have welcomed people from many parts of the Christian spectrum. They have also reached beyond it while staying within the biblical context by including the words of a prominent Hindu, Ashok Bhatt, and of rabbis. (Their own first violinist, Shmuel Ashkenasi, is a Jew.) Some Christians who are given to fences and boundaries have expressed some uneasiness that one of the voices, also on the original CD, is that of a prominent Latter-day Saints leader, Elder Dallin Oaks. But on second thought, they may have been reminded of the way they have listened through the years to radio or television broadcasts which brought them the words and music of the Mormon Tabernacle Choir—words and music that echo their own traditions of hymnody, scripture, and devotion. They may have thus found good reasons to meditate with Dallin Oaks.

Adapting to the many, sometimes controversial voices has demanded growth from all participants, including Richard Young, the editor and main coordinator of the Vermeer performances and of this publication. If all this seems to exemplify what we might call "The Growth of Richard Young," *he* would surely say that it is intended to prod, inspire, and propel *all of us* to enlarge our conceptions and to ready our souls for new experiences.

Certain features leap out at the reader. Take, first, *"Father, forgive them, for they know not what they do."* Who are the "they" who become "them" in that first word? For many centuries, in many places, Christians who read this word or heard it preached knew exactly: "they" were "the Jews," to whom Christian fingers pointed in accusation for what "they" did, as they got blamed for crucifying Jesus.

In the thirteen responses to the first word in this book, the word "Jews" never appears, nor would it have been in place. Often enough through these meditations the word "we" does appear instead. This is because the witnesses who speak and write here, in almost all cases, were part of the group named "we" or "us." They are contemporary believers who acknowledge that their faults make them somehow responsible for the suffering of Jesus, "this amazingly magnanimous Jesus" [Addie Wyatt] who so readily forgives "us."

It may seem harder for "us" to show up in the second word, *"Surely, I say to you, today you will be with me in paradise."* This is because— unless it is being read in a prison, where we hope it will find an audience—few readers of this book or hearers in the various audiences have criminal records. Maybe a teenage adventure or two took them beyond the bounds of the law to what today are called "mistakes," which might mar some citizens' records. But it is a long way from such petty crimes to the violent murders, thefts, or insurrectionary activities that put the two criminals, sometimes called "thieves," on the cross. Certainly, no one today would want to be identified with the crucified thief who, in the story that provides a frame for these words, blasphemed Jesus.

The commentators in this collection, however, would surprise anyone who might wish to keep a distance from this drama and not imagine themselves playing a role in it. Thus the great evangelist Billy Graham assures listeners and readers that the Jesus who answered a criminal's prayer in the Gospel story of long ago will answer *"your"* prayer tonight. Peter Gomes adds that *"we"* are "lost," just as one of the thieves was. Tim Costello points to "the promise that is life eternal for each of us." Others stress that no one, neither the thieves nor any of us, need die alone after Jesus reached out to form a company among the sufferers.

Again, "we" and "us" words pervade the comments, meaning "we," who—as Yvonne Hawkins put it— "mess up so bad."

"Woman, behold your son!" "Behold your mother!" Those two gasps of Jesus that make up the third word from the Cross were uttered to two people: one who had a name, "Mary," and the other who remained nameless, "the disciple whom [Jesus] loved." However, it is hard to picture any unnamed, unidentified believing hearer of this word in our time wanting to be excluded, to be kept at a distance. For that matter, nonbelieving hearers, who are equally welcome and at home in the performances and who might take what they can and wish from these pages, cannot fail to see a working out of a plot that speaks to their lives as well, at least in an indirect and oblique way.

If no one after Good Friday has been called or condemned to *die* alone, as we heard in responses to the second word, in this third word we see Jesus showing concern that those close to him will never have to *live* alone, really alone. In this scene, without benefit of lawyers or courts, we hear of a kind of adoption, the acquiring of a son by a mother, and a mother-equivalent by a disciple. The Mary we have come to recognize in the sculptured Pietas, scenes in which she holds the dead Jesus, must have faced unbearable suffering that night. But profound as her grief must have been, it was somehow bearable, thanks to the care of the disciple. And when the joy of the resurrected presence of Jesus became hers, Mary recognized someone close, the beloved disciple, with whom to share the experience.

Being responsible for the other: that is the theme to which several of the speakers address themselves. Rita Simó had more in mind than just the three characters in this biblical story. Rather, she is saying "Behold!" to "everyone with whom we come in contact, regardless of their color, shape, age, nationality, religion, and even those with whom our country is at war." Michael Pfleger compares those who would wash their hands from responsibility for each other to Pontius Pilate, who washed his in the midst of the proceedings. Gregory Dell contrasts the human disaster that resulted from irresponsibility to the hope that always surprises those who accept responsibility. Finally, John Buchanan shares a painfully "personal anecdote to remind us that [God's] love is intimate and personal."

And so it is with us, in our griefs and our joys alike. "We" are again in this part of the plot. To be hospitable, to open our homes and hearts to others, or to receive hospitality, the gift of openness by others is the great boon that comes with faith in the word voiced by a dying person who had a right to be preoccupied with himself, but instead turned to provide care for someone else.

What can one do with *"Eli, Eli, lama sabachtani? My God, my God, why have you forsaken me?"* This time it would be easy to reduce the cast of characters to two: one of them the very visible dying Jesus, and the other the very remote, hidden, silent One he has often called "Father" but here calls "God." Jesus also calls out to *"my* God." Even in this most agonizing hour of desolation, the bond is not broken. Jesus does not fall silent in abandonment, but with this question protests against it, indicating that the relation with his Father—however strained and however difficult the communication—still offers a chance for him to be heard, to be connected.

Having stressed how the plot involves us, we who may not be the crucifiers or thieves, who are neither the beloved disciple nor the mother of Jesus, come to a point where we cannot include ourselves directly in the drama. This time Jesus' word "my" is unique, intimate, and exclusive— an utterance to God that never needs repeating by any follower. As I wrote in my own meditation on this word, corroborating what other commentators have said, "believers ever since have confidence that he was the *last* one who needed to feel utterly abandoned by God."

Rabbi Peter Knobel, after reflecting on this word that quotes Psalm 22, also finds a way to include "us." "When we forsake each other, we drive God's presence from the world. God is absent when we are absent." Therefore, "we must embrace the pain of others and draw God down from heaven to earth." It turns out that "we" cannot, in the end, be excluded even from this part of the drama of the Seven Last Words.

T. L. Barrett returns to the theme of the believer's relation to the dying Jesus who, though abandoned, did not succumb to despair since he "did not forsake" the God to whom he called out. "Jesus never renounced his embrace, his love, his oneness with his God." Jeremiah Wright reminds us that "*Immanuel* means God is with us—even when we feel abandoned." And Mark Noll, with characteristic evangelical attention to the biblical text behind this word from the Cross, notes that by quoting Psalm 22, Jesus here, and here alone, called out not to "Father" but to "God." And better still for all of us, to "*my* God."

The commentators had and have no difficulty winning empathic responses from listeners and readers to the next word, *"I thirst."* While we are not all in the dramatic cast of the physical crucifiers, the two thieves, the close family members of Jesus, or the abandoned, we all thirst and need relief. As Richard Young puts it in *"The Words and the Music,"* "We can so easily imagine a man who is near death, his strength sapped from him, his throat parched, his tongue like sandpaper, his lips blistering, barely able to choke out the words *'I thirst.'"* Young's explanation of what Haydn does with the music relating to the mere two words "I" and "thirst" makes us thirst to hear it played again. But even more, Young tantalizes us to follow the music and to justify sounds that he describes as "powerful, filled with strength, vitality, and almost defiant self-righteousness."

John Shea elaborates, involving us: "When we are at our end, when our resources seem depleted, when our energies are wasted, when our opportunities are gone, when we reach in the air for we know not what," then Jesus again cries out, and "we are no longer alone. Love, invisible yet real, flows." Thought-provoking similes abound in Dorothy McRae-McMahon's introspective treatment, while Peter Gomes challenges us more directly. He calls this statement of fact about Jesus' thirsty condition "an invitation to respond. To state one's thirst is to invite someone to quench it. Suddenly, we are no longer mere bystanders, voyeurs, and kibbitzers. We are invited, by implication and sympathy, into the narrative."

Dramas move to climaxes and conclusions. *"It is finished!"* the sixth word, signals that this story is soon to end. Raymond Brown has it right when he stresses that Jesus' death "is not only a victorious conclusion but also a beginning." Gilbert Meilaender does not keep himself out of this exchange when he remembers having watched his wife "laboring" to give birth to a child. Suddenly, he says of the painful labor, "it is finished," but "the end of this labor is new life," as in the case of Jesus' fulfillment and the promise of every human child.

Alison Boden ties together the word about "thirst" with this word about finishes and finishing. What was finishing? Among other things, she says, "Finished is the hunger for power that eclipses our thirst for righteousness." There it is again: another "our." Note also that in many of these ten meditations we hear and read of connections between the word "finished" and the word "begun." One such example is Jean Bethke Elshtain's: for her grandfather at the end of his life, as for Jesus at his, "It was finished, only to begin." She is recalling the witness of Dietrich Bonhoeffer, who died condemned by Hitler. His last words were, "This is the end. For me, the beginning of life." That sense of newness was present in a concentration camp. In its own way it has also been evoked in chapels and concert halls where, listening to the music of Haydn, audiences have connected their comings and goings, their ends and beginnings, with the Jesus of this sixth word from the Cross.

What follows seems to be a postscript, a quiet anticlimax. Is that the case of the last word, *"Father, into your hands I commend my spirit"*? Not at all, if we ponder it in context and reread the comments on it. Peter Gomes hears this serene and tranquil word as something congregations sing about in a hymn called "Victory": "The strife is o'er, the battle done." Grover Zinn hears it as "the final secret that Jesus imparts to us," that the strength of faith "leads us through the darkness of death, toward the light of everlasting love."

One voice that does not come from the land of the living is that of Martin Luther King Jr., here transcribed from the Vermeer's recording. This choice is apt, since King was world-renowned for his readiness to "follow" and then to commend his own spirit, as Jesus had, to the one he too often called "Father."

Father Andrew Greeley, one of the most consistent participants in the Vermeer performances, is nationally known as a storyteller. Here in a few lines he has evoked stories from the human condition that soon become reflections of the divine: "The seven last words of Jesus are also *our* seven last words," but words "not without hope." And, finally, Francis Cardinal George cannot resist turning his comment on this word into a prayer: "Lord of life and Lord of death, bring us with you to your Father and ours. Amen."

As someone who pursued his teaching vocation for four decades only two blocks from the chapel in which I have heard the Haydn work and the comments in many different performances, I have often thought of the limits to the meaning of "we" and "our," inclusive words spoken within the community of faith. What do these performances as a whole say to the many who are there as devotees of Haydn and the Vermeer String Quartet, but who come for a performance and emphatically not for worship? They are always encouraged to feel equally welcome at the side of the believers present. There are no faith-security checkers at the door; there is no calling for credentials, no code word passed around for insiders. There is no assumption that everyone present is a believing Christian, or that anyone would become such when "we" are through with them, as if these are evangelistic rallies.

So, what goes on when the general public hears the words gathered here? Let me tell you a story about another occasion at Rockefeller Chapel. A former member of the board of the University of Chicago had died. Through the years I had grown close to his family, who asked me to preach a Christian sermon at his memorial. I was used to the content of many memorial messages delivered at Rockefeller, and had myself delivered some in the semi-secular or secular genre. In many cases, the one being remembered was not an explicit believer and may have been explicitly a nonbeliever. The speaker at such times is sensitive to such a setting and does not violate the integrity, the terms of commitment, of those who come to the memorial service, where either being of faith—one of "us"—or not being such does not matter.

This memorial was different. The family told me that the chapel would be full—it seats well over a thousand—and it was. They told me that prominent Chicagoans and people from around the nation would be there to pay their respects. They would be Protestant, Catholic, Jewish, no doubt Hindu and Muslim, "other," and unidentified or unaffiliated. I was to tell them that the family had asked me to honor their wishes and that of the deceased, and to pretend that this was the little white wooden church "back home" where he grew up and vacationed. So I was to preach a Christian resurrection homily. Which, to the best of my ability, I did.

At a reception following, any number of Jews and self-described nonbelievers made a point of thanking the family for asking me to do this. To summarize the gist of their comments: "Usually we hear Christians at civil or interfaith events, when they are called to accommodate us all, and they are then sensitive. But in the process we never get to hear a focused, rooted, Christian message. For once, we got to learn what it is all about for you Christians, what the attraction is." I doubt there were any unsought conversions that day; I do think there was growth in understanding, in a reach for deeper resources of humanity and our common life.

I have been to events in Japan where the program notes informed me that the story-line connects with Buddhism. I have often been present at Jewish worship and, more recently, at Muslim observances. I go to learn, to enjoy, and to advance understanding. I am not tempted to become a Buddhist, Jew, or Muslim. I would resent any attempt to hold me emotionally captive and to try to convert me. But I also would be frustrated if the hosts, to accommodate me, gave me a watered-down or thinned-out version of their ceremonies.

So it is with the Vermeer Quartet and Haydn, with the speakers and their audiences. In the chapels and auditoriums where the performances have occurred, and from the pages you have just read, you can easily find a focus on "what it is all about," and what believers appreciate. "We" and "our" words mean something different to those worshipping and those enjoying a performance. But on our various levels of engagement, and with respect for the "other" bordering on awe, we all take something profound from the encounter.

Perhaps I have not paid as much attention to the diversity of the people we call "we" at the Vermeer Quartet's presentations here and abroad. The listeners and readers can deduce from their words or see in their brief biographies some of this. Others not featured in these pages have also played key roles. For instance, the Crucifixion by the Romans was in its own way a political event. So, the political world, represented at Vermeer performances by elected officials such as Barack Obama, James Meeks, and Bob Thomas has had its place on the scene. "Peoplehood" could be another category, and Juan Andrade, a leader among Hispanics, embodied one of its many possible ethnic community expressions. Another was Samuel Betances, whose stirring English/Spanish reading of the *Earthquake* text is heard on the CD that accompanies this book. And the Crucifixion, which has inspired so much art and music, quite naturally receives comment from representatives of cultural communities. Some of these included within these pages are Steven Shoemaker, director of the University YMCA in Champaign-Urbana; James Murray, a former choral conductor in Australia; Rita Simó, who founded The People's Music School in inner-city Chicago; and David Neff, who is a choirmaster, organist, and composer in addition to being the editor of *Christianity Today*.

For every Vermeer presentation of Haydn's Good Friday masterpiece at Rockefeller Chapel, I am invited to provide a last printed word in the program. Picture the end of an evening performance, and carry with you the postlude that follows.

POSTLUDE

Martin E. Marty

Now as we go out into the night, we reflect on Jesus' seven cries, related by the Gospel-writers and reflected by Franz Joseph Haydn's music. Inevitably, whether in faith or nonfaith, we see our lives in the light of the remembered experience of those who first heard them.

Some must have walked away in freedom, for Jesus had cried out loud enough that they could hear that they were forgiven. Release, say the forgiven, still occurs.

Perhaps relatives of one dead thief walked home taking comfort from recall of a cry of promise to him. Promises remain compelling.

Jesus' cry had been loud enough for a woman to know she had gained a new son, and for a man to know that he was related to a new mother. Many who hear the story gain new responsibilities.

Jesus' cry of godforsakenness was loud enough, is loud enough, for those who follow him to be assured that no one again need feel, or be, abandoned by God.

Maybe the soldier who now had to rinse out a cup and squeeze out a sponge kept thinking about other things than the cry *"I thirst."* But he had done his duty that day and he had duties now at night. Life goes on. Everyone has duties to attend to.

Anyone who later pondered, could remember the cry announcing that God's work had been completed. This promised a liberating charter for new ways of life. The possibility of newness still beckons.

And those of us who have spirits to commend in hope, have new reasons for doing so. The spirit's search remains urgent.

Ages have passed, and Jesus' seven last words resound not as mere words but as "cries"; announcements, as it were; declarations of his perfect love that still reshapes an imperfect world and many lives within it. Reinforced by Haydn's music, or reinforcing the music, the remembered cries, and the silence that surrounds this love still haunt many and lure more.

NOTES

Notes to A Musical and Spiritual Odyssey,
Pages 1–36

1. Wade Rowland, *Galileo's Mistake—A New Look at the Epic Confrontation between Galileo and the Church* (New York: Arcade Publishing 2003), 266.

2. Paul Hindemith, quoted from memory from material that first appeared in *Neue Musikzeitung*, Regensburg, Germany, 1922.

3. W. Somerset Maugham, *The Moon and Sixpence* (New York: Penguin Books, 1944), 209–10 and 212.

4. Dylan Thomas, *The Collected Poems of Dylan Thomas* (New York: New Directions, 1957), 80.

5. Jane Addams, *Twenty Years at Hull-House* (New York: Macmillan, 1910), 308.

6. Herman Melville, *Moby Dick* (Norwalk, Conn.: Easton Press, 1977), 228–29.

7. Melville, *Moby Dick*, 228.

8. Melville, *Moby Dick*, 443.

9. Martin E. Marty, *A Cry of Absence* (San Francisco: Harper & Row, 1983), 34.

10. *Songs of Zion,* ed. Mada Johnston (hymn collection).

11. Amos Wilder, *The Language of the Gospel: Early Christian Rhetoric* (New York and Evanston: Harper & Row, 1964), 112.

12. Richard John Neuhaus, *The Eternal Pity: Reflections on Dying* (Notre Dame, Ind.: University of Notre Dame Press, 2000), 35.

13. Leo Tolstoy, *The Kreutzer Sonata* (Moscow, USSR: Moskva Hudozhestvenaja Literatura, vol. 10, 1975), 234. (translation) Incidentally, this novel served as the

inspiration for Leoŝ Janácek's first string quartet, an incredibly powerful work whose every measure mirrors Tolstoy's text.

14. Aleksandr Blok, from the translated text for the final movement *(Music)* of a song cycle entitled *Romance-Suite*, Op. 127, composed by Dmitry Shostakovich (Leipzig: VEB Deutscher Verlag für Musik, 1970).

15. Dylan Thomas, preface to *The Collected Poems of Dylan Thomas* (New York: New Directions, 1957).

NOTE TO THE EARTHQUAKE INTRODUCTION, PAGE 155

1. With an occasional word or phrase borrowed from Peter Gomes and Martin Marty.

NOTES TO THE WORDS AND THE MUSIC, PAGES 157–181

1. Portions of *Background, Format, and the Introduction,* plus most of the section on *Woman, behold your son! Behold your mother!* were written by Marc Johnson.

2. Special thanks to Emma Atkins, whose voice is heard on tracks 6 and 7.

3. An interesting parallel—the concept of *tzimtzum*—is described in the meditation by Rabbi Niles Elliot Goldstein on page 109.

4. The other movement is *Surely, I say to you, today you will be with me in paradise,* whose mode change has already been accounted for.

5. It is true that the slow movement of Op. 2 #3 is also muted. However, even though it appears in some editions as a string quartet, this work is actually a divertimento for quartet and two horns.

NOTES TO THE HISTORY OF MEDITATION ON JESUS' SEVEN LAST WORDS, PAGES 183–192

1. Notes. *"When I Survey the Wondrous Cross,"* verse 3.

2. See, for example, the Arundel Psalter, London, British Library, MS Arundel 60, fol. 12v (from Winchester, ca. 1060); a miniature from a Psalter Hymnal painted

by Ingelard of Saint-Germain-des-Prés (Paris), ca. 1030/60, Paris, Bibliothèque National de France, MS lat. 11550, vol. 6r; and an addition from the South of England (second third of eleventh century) to a Gospel Book belonging to Countess Judith of Flanders, New York, Pierpont Morgan Library, MS 709, fol. 1r.

3. On Egeria's travels, with a translation of her letter, see John Wilkinson, *Egeria's Travels,* 3rd ed. (Warminster, England: Aris & Phillips, 1999).

4. See the treatment in John Walton Tyrer, *Historical Survey of Holy Week, Its Services and Ceremonial,* Alcuin Club Collections, no. 29. (London: Oxford University Press, 1932).

5. See the description in Eamon Duffy, *The Stripping of the Altars: Traditional Religion in England, 1400-1580* (New Haven: Yale University Press, 1992), 29–37 and plates 7–10.

6. The origin and spread to Europe and England of the three hours' service are traced by Herbert Thurston, S.J., *Lent and Holy Week: Chapters on Catholic Observance and Ritual* (London: Longmans, Green and Co., 1904). See chapter 9, "The Devotion of the 'Three Hours.'"

7. See G. M. Bosworth, "A Note on the History of the Three-Hour Service," *Church Quarterly Review* 154 (1953): 86–91.

8. W. J. Knox-Little, *The Three Hours' Agony of Our Blessed Redeemer: Addresses in the Form of Meditations,* new ed. (London: Rivingtons, 1889).

9. Niels Krogh Rasmussen, O.P., "Liturgy and Liturgical Arts," in *Catholicism in Early Modern History: A Guide to Research,* vol. 2 of *Reformation Guides to Research* (St. Louis Center for Reformation Research, 1988).

10. James F. White, *Introduction to Christian Worship,* 3rd ed., revised and expanded, (Nashville: Abingdon Press, 2000).

11. *The Book of Worship for Church and Home: With Orders of Worship, Services for the Administration of Sacraments, and Aids to Worship according to the Usages of The Methodist Church* (Nashville: The Methodist Publishing House, 1965).

MISCELLANEOUS NOTE,
PAGE 247

1. Special thanks to Pure Audio (Seattle, Washington) for the recording of *The Introduction,* to WFMT radio for all the other spoken segments, taken from various "live" broadcasts, and to Advanced Audio Technology for the mastering of these CDs.

ABOUT THE
CONTRIBUTORS

Pastor T. L. Barrett is the founder of the Life Center Church of God in Christ on Chicago's South Side. His father died when he was sixteen, and he grew up in one of America's most difficult inner-city environments—the Chicago Housing Authority "projects." And yet, he has become one of the community's most dynamic and influential leaders. Holder of two honorary doctorates and forty-seven civic awards, Pastor Barrett is a board member of the Ministers' Division of Operation PUSH, and conducts a ministry in the Illinois state prison system and in Cook County Jail in Chicago. He is active in the Outreach Ministry for the homeless, the Guardian Angel early intervention program, the Youth for Christ self-help group, the Big Brother/Big Sister adoption program, and the Gang Truce program.

Dr. Samuel Betances is professor emeritus of sociology at Northeastern Illinois University. The recipient of masters and doctorate degrees from Harvard University, he is a founding board member of the Latino Institute and serves as an advisory board member of *Equity and Excellence.* The senior consultant of Souder, Betances, and Associates, Inc., he has worked in every state and territory in the United States, as well as Japan, Korea, Germany, and Mexico, advising presidents, managers, clergy, and educators on workplace diversity issues. He has been honored by the National Puerto Rican Forum, and was given the

Outstanding Leadership Award by the National Alliance of Black School Educators.

Pandit Ashok G. Bhatt is a prominent member of Chicago's Hindu community, having been brought up in a Shiva Temple in the city of Vadodara in Gujarat, India. Since his emigration to the United States in 1967, he has regularly conducted weddings, engagement ceremonies, Satyanarayan pujas, Yagnopavit ceremonies, Nav Chandi Homams, and Mundan ceremonies. An electrical engineer by profession, he is also an accomplished singer of Gujarati folk music, devotional hymns and songs, Hindi ghazals, and light classical music. Six CDs of his lyrics and compositions have been released. A founding member of the India Association of Greater Chicago and the Hindu Cultural Center of Chicago, he is a board member of the Hindu Temple of Greater Chicago, the Chinmaya Mission Chicago, and the Shri Venkateshwara Swami/Balaji temple in Aurora, Illinois.

Tomás Bissonnette is the owner and full-time manager of the Spanish Speaking Bookstore in Chicago, Illinois. A former Catholic priest, he was pastoral assistant in the archdiocese of Detroit and director of religious education at Chicago's St. Jerome Parish. He has also taught at Mercy College in Detroit, the University of Illinois, Chicago, and was director of the Hispanic Institute at Mundelein College. He received a B.A. in philosophy from Sacred Heart College, an M.A. in religious education from Mundelein College, an M.A. in theology from St. John's College in Plymouth, Michigan, and a Ph.D. (A.B.D) in education from the University of Illinois, Chicago.

Rev. Dr. Alison Boden serves as dean of Rockefeller Memorial Chapel and teaches at the University of Chicago's Divinity School. She is a graduate of Vassar College and New York City's Neighborhood Playhouse School of the Theatre. After some years' work as an actress in Manhattan, she began study at the Union Theological Seminary. She received her Ph.D. from the University of Bradford in the United Kingdom. An ordained minister in the United Church of Christ, her past positions include chaplaincies at Bucknell University and Union College. Rev. Boden has been active with a variety of nongovernmental organizations whose focus is religious-based movements for social change in Central America and the Caribbean. She has authored articles on pediatric AIDS, religion and the academy, and human rights in Cuba, as well a book of meditations for Advent: *E'en So, Lord Jesus, Quickly Come.*

Bishop Arthur M. Brazier is the senior pastor of the 18,000-member Apostolic Church of God, located in the Woodlawn community of Chicago, which he has led for more than forty years. While a letter carrier for the U.S. Postal Service, he completed his formal biblical training at the Moody Bible Institute's evening school. He has since received the Rockefeller Service Award from Princeton University as well as honorary doctorates from North Park Seminary, Monrovia College and Industrial Institute, and Mary Holmes College. Committed to improving the quality of life for minorities, Bishop Brazier is the founding chairman of both the Fund for Community Redevelopment and Revitalization and the Woodlawn Preservation and Investment Corporation. A member of the Illinois advisory board of the U.S. Commission on Civil Rights, he was also vice president of the Center for Community Change.

Father Frank Brennan S.J., A.O., is a Jesuit priest and lawyer. He was director of Uniya (the Jesuit Social Justice Centre), an adjunct fellow of the Australian National University in the Research School of Social Sciences, and a member of the Council of the Constitutional Centenary Foundation. He has written extensively on aboriginal land rights, including *One Land, One Nation, Sharing the Country* and *Land Rights, Queensland Style.* In 1989 he won the United Nations Association of Australia Media Peace Award for articles written in support of aboriginal rights, and in 1994 he was named by the National Australia Day Council as an Achiever of the Year. Father Brennan has served as a legal advisor to aboriginal communities and as an aboriginal affairs consultant to the Catholic Bishops of Australia (1985–1992). In 1995 he was made an officer of the Order of Australia (AO) for services to aboriginal Australians, particularly as an advocate in the areas of law, social justice, and reconciliation. In 2004 he began a fellowship at Boston College in America.

Father Raymond E. Brown was called by *Time* magazine "probably the premier Catholic Scripture scholar in the United States." He was the Auburn Distinguished Professor Emeritus of Biblical Studies at Union Theological Seminary. Holder of twenty-four honorary doctorates and a member of the Society of St. Sulpice, he served on the Roman Pontifical Biblical Commission and the International Methodist/Roman Catholic Dialogue. He was a corresponding fellow of the British Academy, the consulter for the Vatican Secretariat for Christian Unity, and the only American Catholic member of the Faith and Order Commission. Author of some twenty books, he was president of the Society of New Testament Studies, the Catholic Biblical Association, and the Society of Biblical Literature.

Dr. John M. Buchanan is the editor of *Christian Century* and the pastor of Chicago's Fourth Presbyterian Church. One of America's most influential Presbyterians, he served as moderator of the 208th General Assembly of the Presbyterian Church U.S.A. Dr. Buchanan received an A.B. in government from Franklin and Marshall College, and the B.D./M.Div. from the University of Chicago Divinity School/Chicago Theological Seminary. He was previously a church pastor in Lafayette (Indiana), Columbus (Ohio), and Dyer (Indiana). He is the chairman of the board of directors of Greater Chicago Broadcast Ministries, and is on the general board of the National Council of Churches. Rev. Buchanan is a member of the board of trustees of Northwestern Memorial Hospital, Presbyterian Homes (Evanston, Illinois), and McCormick Theological Seminary where he was also on the faculty.

Dr. Camilla Burns, S.N.D. de N., was elected in 2002 as the congregational leader of the Sisters of Notre Dame de Namur and is now residing in Rome, Italy. Previously she was the director of the Institute of Pastoral Studies at Loyola University Chicago. She has also taught at Franciscan School of Theology (Berkeley), Holy Names College (Oakland), and Katholieke Universiteit Leuven (Belgium). Her own educational background is an interesting mix of science and religion. At Trinity College and at the University of Notre Dame she earned degrees in mathematics, physics, and chemistry. Later—at Catholic Theological Union, Graduate Theological Union, and Hebrew University in Jerusalem—the emphasis was on biblical studies. Dr. Burns has written many book reviews for *Catholic Biblical Quarterly* and for *Theological Studies*, plus articles for *Bible Today*. She has also authored *Wisdom Tradition in the Old Testament*, six audiocassettes distributed by Alba House Communications.

Rev. Dr. Joan Brown Campbell is the first woman to serve as general secretary of the National Council of Churches. Ordained in 1980, she is a minister in both the Christian Church (Disciples of Christ) and American Baptist Churches in the United States. She is a life member of the NAACP, a board member of Rainbow Push, and was codirector with Rev. Jesse Jackson of the mission to Belgrade, which successfully negotiated the release of American soldiers held captive. Dr. Campbell served as an honorary election monitor in the election of Nelson Mandela in South Africa, and helped negotiate the return of Elian Gonzales to his father in Cuba. The recipient of eleven honorary doctorates, she is a past member of the U.S. State Department advisory committee on Religious Freedom Abroad and serves as trustee for the Council for a Parliament of the World Religions and the Fund for Education in South Africa. She is presently the director of the Department of Religion at the Chautauqua Institution.

Rev. Kelly Clem received a B.A. in psychology from Furman University, an M.Div. from Duke University Divinity School, and an M.A. in counseling from the University of Alabama at Birmingham. She served on the district and conference boards of Ordained Ministry and was on the board of directors of the United Methodist Children's Home in Selma, Alabama. In 1994 Rev. Clem was the pastor of the Goshen United Methodist Church in Piedmont, Alabama, when a tornado struck her church without warning during the Palm Sunday worship service. Kelly, her youngest daughter, and 123 others miraculously survived. Nineteen people were killed, however, including her eldest child, Hannah. Having recently served a missionary with her husband, Dale, in Lithuania through Global Ministries of the United Methodist Church, Kelly is the pastor of a newly formed Methodist church in Huntsville, Alabama.

Rev. Tim Costello studied law at Monash University in Australia, and from 1979 was a solicitor specializing in family and criminal law. He studied theology in Zurich between 1981 and 1984 and during that time was pastor of the Luzern Christian Fellowship. In 1985 he returned to Australia, accepting a call to the St. Kilda Baptist Church. He was ordained as a Baptist minister in 1987. Rev. Costello was the urban mission director for Collins Street Baptist Church, Melbourne, and has been a part-time lecturer in urban missiology and ethics at Whitley Baptist Seminary in Melbourne. In 1999 he formed the Philippines Christian Solidarity Group to raise funds in support of Christians active in human rights in that country. He is now the CEO of World Vision Australia.

Rev. Willie Cusic is manager of the Thelma Marshall Children's Home in Gary, Indiana. He was previously the youth pastor at two South Side Chicago churches, the Second Mt. Vernon Baptist Church and the Zion Hill Missionary Baptist Church. A graduate of Vincennes Junior College and Sangamon State University (where he earned a B.A. degree), he has also attended Northern Baptist Theological Seminary. He has served as executive director of the Ark of St. Sabina Community Ministry and founded a mentoring organization called Men for Children. Rev. Cusic has received numerous awards, including the Martin Luther King award and the Second Congressional Citizen of the Year award. He has devoted his entire adult life to making a difference in the lives of troubled young people—in particular, members of inner-city street gangs.

Rev. Gregory Dell, a United Methodist minister since 1971, has most recently been pastor of the Broadway United Methodist Church in Chicago, Illinois. He is a delegate to that denomination's General Conference and serves on its General Commission on Religion and Race. A graduate of Illinois Wesleyan University and Duke Divinity

School, Rev. Dell has been passionately involved in issues of conscience and social justice. He marched with Dr. King to challenge racism in Chicago neighborhoods and joined the Public Sanctuary Movement on behalf of "illegal refugees from Central America." Honored by the Illinois Coalition for the Homeless, Horizons Chicago, and the Chicago Commission on Human Relations, he is director of *In All Things Charity*. In 1999 his ordination credentials were temporarily suspended for conducting a Service of Holy Union for two gay men.

Father Virgil P. Elizondo was the founder and first president of both the Mexican American Cultural Center and the Incarnate Word College Pastoral Institute in San Antonio, Texas. The former rector of San Fernando Cathedral, he is best known to millions of Hispanic Americans as the host, executive producer, and founder of *Nuestra Santa Misa de las Americas,* an international weekly televised mass for the Americas. He has degrees from the Institut Catholique (Paris), Ateneo University (Manila), the East Asian Pastoral Institute, and St. Mary's University. He has also been awarded the Laetare Medal, the University of Notre Dame's highest honor for his "contributions to humanity," and the Quasten Medal of the Catholic University of America for "creative contribution to theology." A number of his influential books are widely used in major universities throughout the world. Father Elizondo has taught at the University of Notre Dame and Union Theological Seminary, and has been named to *Time* magazine's list of "100 innovators in religion."

Dr. Jean Bethke Elshtain is the Laura Spelman Rockefeller Professor of Social and Political Ethics at the University of Chicago. She has been a fellow at the Institute for Advanced Study and the National Humanities Center, a Phi Beta Kappa Scholar, and a Guggenheim Fellow. Elected to the American Academy of Arts and Sciences in 1996, she has chaired the Council on Civil Society and has been codirector of the Pew Forum on Religion and Public Life. In 2003 she was named the second Carey McGuire Chair in Ethics at the Library of Congress. Her many books include *Democracy on Trial* (1995); *Augustine and the Limits of Politics* (1996); *Real Politics: At the Center of Everyday Life* (1997); *New*

221

Wine and Old Bottles: International Ethics at Century's End (1998); *Who Are We? Critical Reflections, Hopeful Possibilities* (the American Society of Theological Booksellers' best book of 2000); *Jane Addams and the Dream of American Democracy* (2001); and *Just War against Terror: The Burden of American Power in a Violent World* (2002).

Francis Cardinal George, O.M.I., is the Catholic archbishop of Chicago, having previously served as Archbishop of Portland, Oregon. He received a B.Th. and M.A. (theology) from the University of Ottawa, an M.A. (philosophy) from the Catholic University of America, a Ph.D. (American philosophy) from Tulane University, and an S.T.D. (ecclesiology) from Pontifical University Urbaniana. Cardinal George has taught at Tulane, Our Lady of the Lake, Gonzaga, and Creighton universities, as well as Oblate Seminary. A member of the National Conference of Catholic Bishops, he is chancellor of the Catholic Church Extension Society and the University of St. Mary of the Lake. A trustee of the Papal Foundation, he is a member of the Board of Trustees of the Catholic University of America and of the National Shrine of the Immaculate Conception.

Rabbi Niles Elliot Goldstein is the founding rabbi of the New Shul, an innovative and independent congregation in Greenwich Village, New York. He is an associate faculty member of the National Jewish Center for Learning and Leadership, where he was the Steinhardt Senior Fellow. He is a member of the Renaissance Institute and a former congregational rabbi in New Rochelle, New York. Rabbi Goldstein is the author or editor of six books: *Lost Souls: Finding Hope in the Heart of Darkness; God at the Edge: Searching for the Divine in Uncomfortable and Unexpected Places; Spiritual Manifestos: Visions for Renewed Religious Life in America from Young Spiritual Leaders of Many Faiths; Forests of the Night: The Fear of God in Early Hasidic Thought; Judaism and Spiritual Ethics;* and *Duties of the Soul: The Role of Commandments in Liberal Judaism.* The voice behind "Ask the Rabbi" on the Microsoft Network, he lectures frequently on issues in mysticism and spirituality as well as on new models for religious life in the twenty-first century.

Rev. Professor Peter J. Gomes is a member of the faculty of Arts and Sciences and of the faculty of Divinity of Harvard University. An American Baptist minister, he holds degrees from Bates College (A.B., 1965) and the Harvard Divinity School (S.T.B, 1968), and twenty-one honorary degrees. He is an honorary fellow of Emmanuel College, the University of Cambridge, England, where the Gomes Lectureship is established in his name, and member of the Council of Sarum College, Salisbury Cathedral, England. Named Clergy of the Year in 1998 by *Religion in American Life,* he participated in the presidential inaugurations of Ronald Reagan and George Herbert Walker Bush. His recent best-selling books include *A Call to Heroism: Renewing America's Vision of Greatness* (2002), and *Strength for the Journey: Biblical Wisdom for Daily Living* (2003). Profiled in *The New Yorker* and on *60 Minutes,* Dr. Gomes was named in 1999 by *Talk* magazine one of "The Best Talkers in America: Fifty Big Mouths We Hope Will Never Shut Up."

Mary Gonzales is the director of the Metropolitan Alliance of Congregations, an institutionally based community organization that reaches some 300 congregations in the metropolitan Chicago area. The MAC endeavors to bring about needed change in public policy, affecting the economic circumstances of scores of underserved communities. Since 1987 Ms. Gonzales has worked to improve the quality of life for these residents by focusing on education, decent housing, meaningful jobs, and neighborhood safety. Through her association with the Gamaliel Foundation, she has trained clergy and lay leaders throughout the United States. She has also done similar work in the Natal Province of South Africa. She is a Mexican-American Chicago native, married, and the mother of four daughters.

Evangelist Billy Graham has preached to more people in live audiences than anyone in history—more than 180 million people in more than 180 countries and territories. Dr. Graham's weekly "Hour of Decision" radio program has been broadcast to more than 700 stations around the world, and his newspaper column, "My Answer," has been carried by newspapers with a combined circulation of 5 million readers. His

Decision magazine is read in 158 countries and has a circulation of nearly 2 million. Dr. Graham has written seventeen books, all of which have become top sellers. He has been regularly listed by the Gallup organization as one of the "Ten Most Admired Men in the World," and was described by them as the dominant figure in that survey over the past five decades. His stirring telling of the story of "the thief on the cross"—included in both the Vermeer Quartet's CD as well as this collection of meditations—was taken from a sermon entitled "The Cross of Christ," delivered in 1972 at Legion Field in Birmingham, Alabama.

Father Andrew M. Greeley is professor of social sciences at the University of Chicago and the University of Arizona, as well as research associate at the National Opinion Research Center. He received an S.T.L. from St. Mary of the Lake Seminary, and an M.A. and Ph.D. from the University of Chicago. The author of scores of books and hundreds of popular and scholarly articles, Father Greeley has also written more than thirty best-selling novels. His column on church, political, and social issues is carried by the New York Times Religious News Service. He has established a $1 million Catholic Inner-City School Fund, a chair in Roman Catholic Studies at the University of Chicago, and an annual lecture series at St. Mary of the Lake Seminary. His most recent books include *Furthermore! Memoirs of a Parish Priest.*

Stan Guthrie is the associate news editor of *Christianity Today.* He was formerly the managing editor for the Evangelism and Missions Information Service, a department of the Billy Graham Center at Wheaton College. He is also managing editor of *Evangelical Missions Quarterly,* the editor of *World Pulse,* and the editor of *Discernment,* the newsletter of Wheaton College's Center for Applied Christian Ethics. A member of the National Association of Evangelicals, the Evangelical Missiological Society, and the Evangelical Press Association, his "Global Report" column appears in *EMQ.* Mr. Guthrie earned a B.S. degree in journalism from the University of Florida (Gainesville), and an M.A. in missions from Columbia International University (South Carolina). He is coauthor of *Disciplining Nations: The Power of Truth to Transform*

Cultures, a contributor to the *Evangelical Dictionary of World Missions,* and the author of *Missions in the Third Millennium.*

Rev. Yvonne D. Hawkins has been an associate minister at Park Manor Christian Church on Chicago's South Side. She was also the on-call chaplain at Children's Memorial Hospital, and taught at the Sankofa School at St. John AME Church in Aurora, Illinois. In addition she worked at Evanston Hospital in the AIDS Pastoral Care Network and at Chicago's Good News Community Church. As an outreach minister at Union Missionary Baptist Church in Lansing, Michigan, she focused on the prison and domestic abuse shelter ministries. Rev. Hawkins received an M.Div. from Garrett-Evangelical Theological Seminary as well as a B.S. from Northwestern University's Medill School of Journalism. She was a news editor for the *Lansing State Journal* and a reporter and copy editor for *The Herald-Dispatch* in Huntington, West Virginia. She is currently the editor of the *Sioux Falls Business Journal* in South Dakota where she is also an associate minister at Friendship Baptist Church.

Rabbi Daniel Isaak is the senior rabbi of Congregation Neveh Shalom in Portland, Oregon, having previously served at Congregation Sons of Israel in Briarcliff Manor, New York, and Temple Beth El in Hackensack, New Jersey. He holds a B.A. from the University of California at Berkeley as well as masters and doctorate degrees from the Jewish Theological Seminary of America. He also pursued his education at Hebrew University in Jerusalem. Rabbi Isaak is a member of the Rabbinical Assembly of America and was the president of both the Ossining Ministerial Association and the Oregon Board of Rabbis. He is a member of the Interreligious Committee for Peace in the Middle East and serves on the board of the American Friends of Peace Now and the Hopewell House Residential Hospice.

Marc Johnson is the cellist of the Vermeer String Quartet. He studied in Lincoln, Nebraska, with Carol Work, at the Eastman School of Music with Ronald Leonard, and at Indiana University with Janos Starker and Josef Gingold. While still a student, he was the youngest member of the

Rochester Philharmonic, and has subsequently performed as soloist with that orchestra. In addition to numerous other awards, he won first prize in the prestigious Washington International Competition. Before joining the Vermeer, Mr. Johnson was a member of the Pittsburgh Symphony Orchestra. He has recorded for CRI records and has received critical acclaim for his recitals and solo appearances with various orchestras in the United States and Europe. A fellow of the Royal Northern College of Music in Manchester, England, he is a professor at Northern Illinois University where the Vermeer is the quartet-in-residence.

Very Rev. Father Demetri C. Kantzavelos is the chancellor of the Metropolis of Chicago of the Greek Orthodox Church. He previously served as an associate pastor of Annunciation Cathedral of Chicago. He attended Hellenic College, received his graduate divinity degree from Holy Cross Seminary, and pursued postgraduate work at Loyola University's doctoral philosophy program. Father Demetri participated in the Orthodox-Lutheran and Orthodox-Roman Catholic Dialogue Commissions, the NCCJ, the Orthodox caucus of the National Council of Churches of Christ, the Illinois Council of Churches, the Council of Religious Leaders of Metropolitan Chicago, the Annual Christian-Jewish Clergy Retreat, and the Council for a Parliament of the World's Religions. He is the founder of the Bishop's Task Force on AIDS, has been an important advocate for death row inmates, and is president of the Illinois Coalition against the Death Penalty.

Rev. Jarrett Kerbel is an Episcopal priest and rector of St. Mary's Church in Park Ridge, Illinois. He was previously the associate rector of St. Paul and the Redeemer Episcopal Church in Hyde Park, Illinois. A graduate of Union Theological Seminary in New York City, he has ministered in rural, urban, and suburban churches, worked as a hospital chaplain, and taught Head Start. He serves on the board of the Chicago Inter-Faith Committee for Workers Issues. His passion is building strong congregations that use their energy to work for justice and reconciliation in the world. Jarrett is somewhat unique in the Episcopal Church: a thirty-six-year-old priest with a decade of ordained experience. He is married to Rev. Alison Boden and has two young children, Timothy and Martha.

Rev. Martin Luther King Jr. is one of the most important figures in American history. His meditation on "Father, into your hands I commend my spirit" that is heard on the Vermeer Quartet's CD of *The Seven Last Words of Christ* (and which is included in *this* collection) is from a sermon entitled "Garden of Gethsemane." This was delivered in 1957 when Rev. King was twenty-eight years old—nine years after his ordination and his graduation from Morehouse College, six years after graduating from Crozer Theological Seminary, four years after marrying Coretta Scott, three years after *Brown vs. Board of Education*, two and a half years after earning a Ph.D. from Boston University and becoming pastor of Dexter Avenue Baptist Church in Montgomery, sixteen months after the protest by Rosa Parks, two months after being elected president of the Southern Christian Leadership Conference, six years before his "I Have a Dream" speech, and eleven years before he was assassinated.

Rabbi Peter S. Knobel is the rabbi at Beth Emet the Free Synagogue in Evanston, Illinois, where he has served since 1980. He received his graduate degree from Hebrew Union College and his Ph.D. from Yale University, and has taught at Hebrew Union College, Spertus College, Yale University, New Haven College, and the University of Connecticut. The past president of the Chicago Board of Rabbis and the Chicago Association of Reform Rabbis, Rabbi Knobel has been a member of the Illinois State Attorney's Task Force "Foregoing of Life Sustaining Treatment." He has published papers and articles on such subjects as assisted suicide, Zionism, Reform Judaism, dietary laws, spirituality, rites of passage in Judaism, homosexuality, and is currently working on a new siddur while serving as chair of the Liturgy Committee for the Central Conference of American Rabbis.

Dr. Robert Ludwig is director of the Institute of Pastoral Studies at Loyola University Chicago. He was formerly director of University Ministry and professor of Catholic Studies at DePaul University in Chicago, Illinois, as well as director of the Loyola Institute for Ministry at Loyola University, New Orleans. He holds a bachelor's degree in philosophy from Loras College in Dubuque, Iowa, and an M.A. and Ph.D.

in theological studies from the Aquinas Institute of Theology. Dr. Ludwig is the author of the award-winning book *Reconstructing Catholicism for a New Generation* (Crossroad, 1995). He is coeditor with Jeffrey Carlson of *Jesus and Faith: A Conversation on the Work of John Dominic Crossan* (Orbis, 1994). His biographical essay on Msgr. John Egan appears in the memorial edition of *An Alley In Chicago: The Life and Legacy of Msgr. John Egan* (Sheed & Ward, 2002).

Pastor B. Herbert Martin Sr. is pastor of Chicago's Progressive Community Center—The People's Church. He is a member of the Human Services Reform Task Force for the State of Illinois, as well as a founding member of the Congregation and Residents Together Initiative. He was also the executive director of the Chicago Commission on Human Relations, the chairman of the Chicago Housing Authority, and the president of the Southside Branch of the NAACP. Pastor Martin has taught at the Seminary Consortium of Urban Pastoral Education, the Chicago Christian Laity, the Northern Baptist Theological Seminary, the University of Tel Aviv, the University of Illinois, and the University of Chicago Divinity School. In 1995 he was inducted into the Martin Luther King Jr. International Board of Preachers at Morehouse College in Atlanta.

Dr. Martin E. Marty is the Fairfax M. Cone Distinguished Service Professor Emeritus at the University of Chicago where he taught for thirty-five years and where the Martin Marty Center has since been founded. He was the founding president of the Park Ridge Center for Health, Faith, and Ethics and is now the George B. Caldwell Senior Scholar-in-Residence there. Dr. Marty has been awarded the National Humanities Medal, the Order of Lincoln Medallion (Illinois' top honor), the Medal of the American Academy of Arts and Sciences, the National Book Award (for *Righteous Empire*), and seventy honorary doctorates. He has been president of the American Academy of Religion, the American Society of Church History, and the American Catholic Historical Association. He has written more than fifty books, including *The One and the Many: America's Search for the Common Good; Education, Religion, and the Common Good; Politics, Religion, and the*

Common Good; and the three-volume *Modern American Religion.* His most recent book is *Martin Luther* (Penguin Lives series, Viking Penguin, 2004).

Rev. Landis H. McAlpin is the Protestant chaplain of the Chicago Fire Department. He attended Paine College in Augusta, Georgia, Moody Bible Institute, Spertus College of Judaica, and earned a M.Div. degree from Chicago Theological Seminary. As the only African American to serve as a trustee on the executive board of the Fire-Fighters Union, Local 2, Rev. McAlpin helped secure their first labor contract with the city of Chicago. He was also appointed to the Management Oversight Review Committee of the Chicago Housing Authority in 1983. In addition Rev. McAlpin has served as chairman of the Ecumenical Events Committee of the Church Federation of Greater Chicago. He retired as Chicago Fire Department Chaplain in 1990 after ten years of service, only to return in 1998 at the request of Fire Commissioner Altmann.

Dr. Dorothy McRae-McMahon was born in Tasmania, Australia. She has been awarded the Australian Government Peace Award, the Australian Human Rights Medal, the Jubilee Medal for work with women in New South Wales, and an Honorary Doctorate of Letters from Macquarie University for work with Australian minorities. Her most recent books include *Daring Leadership in the 21st Century* (ABC Books, 2001) and *Rituals for Life, Love and Loss* (Jane Curry, 2003). She has worked as a preschool teacher, as staff member of the New South Wales Ecumenical Council, as a parish minister with the Pitt Street Uniting Church in Sydney, and as national director for Mission of the Uniting Church in Australia. She retired from this position after informing her church she is a lesbian. In 2003 that church approved the ordination of homosexual clergy.

Dr. Gilbert C. Meilaender Jr. holds the Richard and Phyllis Duesenberg Chair in Christian Ethics at Valparaiso University. He earned a B.A. from Concordia Senior College, an M.Div. from Concordia Seminary, and a Ph.D. from Princeton University. He has previously taught at the University of Virginia and Oberlin College. Dr. Meilaender has been on the editorial boards of the *Journal of Religious Ethics*, the *Annual of Society of Religious Ethics*, and *Dialog*. He has also been the associate editor of both the *Journal of Religious Ethics* and *Religious Studies Review.* His most recent books are *Things That Count: Essays Moral and Theological* (ISI Books, 2000) and *Working: Its Meaning and Its Limits* (University of Notre Dame Press, 2000). A board member of the Society of Christian Ethics, Dr. Meilaender is part of the President's Council on Bioethics.

Father Gary Miller was ordained a priest for the archdiocese of Chicago in 1972 and is now the pastor of St. Bernadette Parish in Evergreen Park. He received a B.A. in philosophy in 1968 and an M.Div. in 1972 from St. Mary of the Lake Seminary in Mundelein, Illinois. He served in various parishes as an associate pastor for seventeen years. Father Miller was appointed pastor of Chicago's St. Pascal Catholic Church in 1989, which is where he collaborated with the Vermeer Quartet in a performance of Haydn's *The Seven Last Words of Christ* in 1995.

Rev. Leroy A. Mitchell is founder and pastor of the New Hope Missionary Baptist Church in DeKalb, Illinois. He is also the associate director of educational services and programs at Northern Illinois University and the director of CHANCE, an educational opportunity program that recruits, admits, and provides support services for underprivileged minority students. Originally from White Plains, New York, he earned B.S.Ed. and M.S.Ed. degrees from State University College at Buffalo. He received his M.Div. from Northern Baptist Theological Seminary in Lombard, Illinois. Rev. Mitchell previously taught at Herbert Hoover Junior High School in Kenmore, New York, and was director of special academic programs at Canisius College in Buffalo.

Father James Murray is a graduate of Scotch College in Melbourne, Australia. Trained in choral conducting by Professor John Bishop, he was prominent in school music in the 1950s and was ordained to the Anglican priesthood in 1962. As chaplain to Victoria's Social Welfare Department, he worked in remand centers and at Pentridge Gaol. These experiences led to a book, *Sprung: A Study in Victims*. Moving to Sydney, he assisted at St. James' Church, King Street, and continued teaching in the 1960s. In 1969 he became religious affairs writer for the country's leading newspaper, *The Australian*. His books include *Larrikins, The Mask of Time, An Illustrated History of Sidney*; *The Paradise Tree*; and *Would You Believe?*, interviews with leading Australians on faith and doubt. He is a member of Societas Sanctae Crucis, the Society of the Holy Cross.

David Neff is the editor of *Christianity Today* magazine and editorial vice president of *Christianity Today, International*. Mr. Neff graduated from Loma Linda University in 1969 and Andrews University in 1973, and did additional graduate study at San Francisco Theological Seminary. Prior to entering the publishing field, Mr. Neff was a campus pastor and religion teacher at Walla Walla College. Before coming to *Christianity Today* in 1985, he served as editor of *HIS*, InterVarsity Christian Fellowship's erstwhile magazine for college students. He was also involved as business and promotion manager for the launch of the *Journal of Christian Nursing* for Nurses Christian Fellowship. As the organist/choirmaster at St. Barnabas Episcopal Church in Glen Ellyn, Illinois, he has composed new music and written new tunes for older hymn texts.

Professor Mark A. Noll is McManis Professor of Christian Thought and Professor of History at Wheaton College where he has taught since 1979. He has a B.A. degree in English from Wheaton College, an M.A. in comparative literature from the University of Iowa, an M.A. in church history from Trinity Evangelical Divinity School, and a Ph.D. in American religious history from Vanderbilt University. He was the inaugural McDonald Family Visiting Professor of Evangelical Theological Studies at the Harvard Divinity School. He is a member of the American Historical Association, the American Society of Church History, and is an advisory editor for *Books and Culture: A Christian Review*. His most recent books include *The Work We Have to Do: A History of Protestants in America* (2nd ed., Oxford University Press, 2002), *The Old Religion in a New World: The History of North American*

Christianity (Eerdmans, 2002), and *America's God, from Jonathan Edwards to Abraham Lincoln* (Oxford University Press, 2002).

Dr. Dallin H. Oaks is a member of the council of the Twelve Apostles of the Church of Jesus Christ of Latter-day Saints. In addition to degrees from Brigham Young University and the University of Chicago Law School, he has received honorary doctorates from Pepperdine, Brigham Young, and Southern Utah universities. A former law clerk to Chief Justice Earl Warren of the U.S. Supreme Court, he was a justice of the Utah Supreme Court. He has served as acting dean of the University of Chicago Law School, and was president of Brigham Young University. Besides seven law books and more than 100 legal articles, Elder Oaks is the author of two books and numerous articles and published sermons on LDS church doctrine and practice.

Rev. John C. Ortberg Jr. is pastor of Menlo Park Presbyterian Church in San Francisco, California. When he appeared with the Vermeer Quartet at the University of Chicago in 2001, he was a teaching pastor at Willow Creek Community Church where he served for nine years. Located in South Barrington, Illinois, Willow Creek is one of the largest Christian churches in America. Its focus is Evangelism, and each week more than 17,000 people attend. Rev. Ortberg received an M.Div. and a Ph.D. in clinical psychology at Fuller Theological Seminary in Pasadena where he also serves on the board of trustees. The author of *The Life You've Always Wanted* (Zondervan 1997) and *Love Beyond Reason* (Zondervan 1998), he has also written various articles on psychology and ministry. Rev. Ortberg and his wife Nancy have three children, Laura, Mallory, and Johnny.

Rev. Donald L. Parson is pastor of the 2,500-member Logos Baptist Assembly on Chicago's South Side. The son of a Baptist minister, he preached as "the boy evangelist" at numerous revivals. At age nineteen he became pastor of the Jerusalem Baptist Church in Gary, Indiana, then later moved to Chicago to be pastor of Mt. Calvary Baptist Church. Under his leadership Chicago's largest Sunday school was built, and church membership grew from a few hundred to almost 5,000. In

1991 Rev. Parson organized Logos Baptist Assembly, whose services are broadcast over WYBA radio and WJYS television. A frequent preacher at the National Baptist Convention of America, he was an organizer of Operation Breadbasket, a founding member of the National Black Pastor's Association, and chairman of the Minister's Division of Operation Push.

Rev. Michael L. Pfleger is pastor of St. Sabina Catholic Church on Chicago's South Side. He has earned degrees at the University of St. Mary of the Lake and Loyola University, and has completed postgraduate studies at Mundelein College and the Catholic Theological Union. A Chicago native, Rev. Pfleger has lived and ministered in African American neighborhoods since 1968. He has received dozens of awards for his work as a community activist devoted to addressing problems of gangs, violence, homelessness, drugs, alcohol, and the economic exploitation of minorities. In 2001, Father Pfleger was a key figure in the bitter dispute involving St. Sabina's membership in a predominately white sports league for teenagers. This protracted high-profile controversy shed considerable light on Chicago's evolving race relations.

233

Dr. John Shea is a theologian and storyteller who lectures nationally and internationally. He has been a research professor of systematic theology and the director of the Doctor of Ministry program at the University of St. Mary of the Lake, as well as a research professor at the Institute of Pastoral Studies at Loyola University of Chicago. In addition he has been the Advocate Healthcare Senior Scholar in Residence at the Park Ridge Center for the Study of Health, Faith, and Ethics where he has created programs of spiritual development for older Americans. Dr. Shea has also taught at the University of Notre Dame and Boston College. A recipient of the John XXIII Award, he has published eleven books of theology and two books of poetry. His latest book is *Spirituality and Health Care: Reaching Toward a Holistic Future* (Park Ridge Center, 2000).

Rev. Steven Shoemaker is the executive director of the University YMCA at the University of Illinois, Champaign-Urbana. A Presbyterian minister with two graduate degrees from McCormick Theological Seminary in Chicago, he served as pastor/director of McKinley Presbyterian Church/McKinley Foundation at the University of Illinois from 1981 to 1999, and as Presbyterian campus minister at North Carolina State University from 1973 to 1981. A graduate of Wheaton College, he has a Ph.D. in religion from Duke University and has taught at Parkland College and the University of Illinois. His poems, articles, reviews, sermons, and letters have been published in *Judaism, The National Catholic Reporter, The American Scholar, The Christian Century, The Christian Ministry, The Journal of the American Academy of Religion, The Anglican Theological Review, Religion in Life, Books & Religion, The Presbyterian Outlook,* and the *Presbyterian Survey.*

Rita Simó is the founder and director emeritus of the People's Music School in Chicago's Uptown neighborhood. A Dominican Republic native, she won a piano scholarship to Juilliard and vowed to "pay back" by one day opening a tuition-free music school for disadvantaged American children. She received a doctorate from Boston University, taught at Rosary College, and joined the Sinsinawa Dominican religious order, but resigned to devote all her energies to her inner-city dream. Her school opened in 1976 in a rented storefront with a faculty of three. In 1995 it moved to its impressive new facility, built on an abandoned city lot next to a halfway-house, on a street that has since been named Rita Simó Way. Dr. Simó has transformed the lives of countless people by offering not only "the gift of music," but by stressing individual and community responsibility.

Rev. William B. Spofford was the fourth bishop of Diocese of Eastern Oregon, and the assistant bishop of the Diocese of Washington, D.C., where he presided at the National Cathedral. Prior to his election as bishop, he was dean of St. Michael's Cathedral in Boise, Idaho, and the supervisory chaplain of Massachusetts General Hospital in Boston and McLean Hospital in Belmont, Massachusetts. His avocational interests are theater, poetry, training persons for ministry, and mountain hiking. He is a graduate of Antioch College, the Episcopal Divinity School, and the University of Michigan School of Social Work. He did his clinical pastoral education at the Menninger Clinic in Topeka, Kansas. When he appeared with the Vermeer Quartet in 1997, he was the pastor of Grace Memorial Episcopal Church in Portland, Oregon.

Dick Staub is the founder of the Center for Faith and Culture, which helps people understand and communicate their beliefs in the context of popular culture. Since 1987 he has been host of *The Dick Staub Show*, a popular radio program that features lively, interactive discussion on current events from a broad Christian perspective. Syndicated by the Salem Radio Network and heard over forty stations nationwide, it has won many honors including the Cardinal's Award for Excellence in Broadcasting. Mr. Staub graduated cum laude from Simpson College (B.A.) and Gordon-Conwell Seminary (M.Div.), and pursued further studies at Harvard University and the University of Washington. The author of *Too Christian, Too Pagan* and the coauthor of *Career Kit*, he has written articles for *Christianity Today, Christian Reader, Moody Magazine, World Christian*, and *Books & Culture*. Now living in Seattle, Mr. Staub has been a featured speaker at dozens of colleges, seminaries, and workshops.

Dr. Elizabeth-Anne Stewart has taught English at DePaul University, graduate religious studies at Mundelein College, and poetry at Express-Ways Children's Museum. She has written articles on liturgy, scripture, spirituality, and creativity for various religious journals and has given workshops on creative writing and religious topics to faculties and church groups. She has been a poetry advisor to the International Commission on English in the Liturgy's subcommittee on the liturgical psalter. She has earned B.A. and M.A. degrees in English from the University of Malta and DePaul University, plus a D.Min. from the Graduate Theological Foundation and a Ph.D. in theology from the University of Malta. She is the author of three poetry collections and several books, including *From Center to Circumference: God's Place in the Circle of Self* and *Pilgrams at Heart*.

Lydia Talbot is the executive director of the Greater Chicago Broadcast Ministries, which continues a forty-six-year history of television programming in Chicago on matters of faith and culture. She has been writing, editing, producing, and hosting award-winning television programs for more than thirty years. She is the permanent host of *30 Good Minutes* on public television and *Sanctuary* on ABC. Ms. Talbot is chair of the Chicago Sunday Evening Club Board of Trustees and a board member of both *Christian Century* magazine and the Mid-America Leadership Foundation. In 2001 she received the Gutenberg Award from the Chicago Bible Society. Other honors include a Chicago Television Emmy Award, plus the Board of Governors Award of the City Club of Chicago for outstanding contribution to human relations through public service television.

Rev. Rachel Thompson is the minister for congregational life at Bedford Presbyterian Church in Bedford, New York. She graduated from Union Theological Seminary in May 2002, having previously earned a B.A. in theater from the University of California at Berkeley and an M.S. in communications from the University of Illinois. She has also worked as a commercial photographer, a freelance writer/editor, and a performing arts marketing director. It was when she was pursuing her studies at Union Theological Seminary in 1997 that she participated in a Vermeer performance of *The Seven Last Words of Christ* at Columbia University in New York.

Dr. Edgar T. Thornton was pastor of the Original Providence Baptist Church on Chicago's West Side from 1958 until his retirement in 1997. He served as a pastor in Illinois, Ohio, Virginia, and Kansas for more than a half a century. He has degrees from Southern University, Oberlin College, Roosevelt University, Vanderbilt University, Central Baptist Theological Seminary, and the University of Sarasota. The recipient of numerous community awards, Dr. Thornton served for twenty-four years in the human relations department of the Chicago Board of Education. He has taught at McCormick Theological Seminary, Governors State University, Malcolm X College, and Roosevelt University. He was also a high school principal in Vidalia (Louisiana), dean of Virginia Theological Seminary and College, and president of Western Baptist Seminary.

Dr. David Tracy is the Andrew Thomas Greeley and Grace McNichols Greeley Distinguished Service Professor of Theology at the University of Chicago Divinity School, where he has taught since 1969. A professor in the Committee on the Analysis of Ideas and Methods and in the Committee on Social Thought, he has also lectured at dozens of institutions throughout the world. Dr. Tracy holds a licentiate in theology and a doctorate in theology from Gregorian University in Rome, plus six honorary doctorates. He is a member of the American Academy of Arts and Sciences, the American Academy of Religion, and is the past president of the Catholic Theological Society of America. Among his recent books are *Plurality and Ambiguity: Hermeneutics, Religion and Hope* (1987), *Dialogue with the Other* (1990), and *Naming the Present* (1995).

Sister Evelyn Varboncoeur, S.S.C.M., has been the board chair of the Provena Covenant Medical Center in Urbana, Illinois, since 1996. From 1977 to 1991 she held the same position at St. Mary's Hospital in Kankakee, Illinois, having previously served as the hospital's assistant administrator from 1971 to 1977. Sister Evelyn received a B.S. in medical technology from St. Louis University in 1961, and an M.S. in microbiology from Catholic University in 1964. From 1964 to 1970 she was a medical technologist in the laboratory of St. Mary's Hospital. Since taking her final vows in her religious community in 1962, most of her years in ministry have been devoted to health care governance. Since the mid-1960s she has served on the boards of ServantCor and Provena Health. From 1991 to 1996 she was the assistant to her community's General Superior in Montreal. She is a member of Zonta International and an active member of St. Mary Parish in Champaign, Illinois.

Rev. Allan B. Warren III is the XV rector of the Church of the Advent in Boston, Massachusetts. A native of Virginia, he received his A.B. *magna cum laude* from Princeton in 1969, and received his S.T.B degree from General Theological Seminary in New York in 1972. He served at parishes in South Carolina and New York City until 1981 when he was appointed canon pastor at the American Cathedral in Paris. From 1984 to 1990 he was rector of the Church of the Good Shepherd in Waban, and in 1990 was appointed assistant to the rector at the Church of the Advent. From 1993 until 1999 he was rector of the Church of the Resurrection in Manhattan.

Bishop Rembert G. Weakland, O.S.B., is the Catholic Archbishop Emeritus of Milwaukee, having been appointed to that position in 1977 by Pope Paul VI. His theological studies were done at the International Benedictine College of Sant'Anselmo in Rome, and at St. Vincent Seminary in Pennsylvania. He later studied music in Italy, France, Germany, and New York—at Columbia University and the Juilliard School of Music. Father Weakland has been chairman of the National Conference of Catholic Bishops' ad hoc Committee on Catholic Social Teaching and the U.S. Economy, the NCCB Committee on the Liturgy, and the NCCB Committee for Ecumenical and Interreligious Affairs. He also served as cochairman of its Dialogue and Theological Consultation between the Roman Catholic and Eastern Orthodox Churches.

Rev. Dr. Vincent L. Wimbush is a professor at the School of Religion of Claremont Graduate University in California. He previously taught at Union Theological Seminary and Columbia University in New York. He received his M.Div. in 1978 from Yale University Divinity School and his Ph.D. in 1983 from Harvard University Graduate School of Arts and Sciences. Works he has edited include *Ascetic Behavior in Greco-Roman Antiquity: A Source Book* (1990) and *Discursive Formations, Ascetic Piety, and the Interpretation of Early Christian Literature* (1992). He has written articles for *Harper's Encyclopedia for Religious Education, Theology Today, Journal of Feminist Studies in Religion,* and *Theological Education,* among others. His most recent book is *The Bible and African-Americans: A Brief History* (2003).

Rev. Jeremiah A. Wright Jr. is pastor of the 7,000-member Trinity United Church of Christ on Chicago's South Side. He holds a D.Min. from United Theological Seminary, M.A. degrees from Howard University and the University of Chicago, and three honorary doctorates. Pastor Wright has taught at Chicago Theological Union, LaVern

University, North Park Theological Seminary, Catholic Theological Union, the Chicago Center for Black Religious Studies, and the Seminary Consortium for Urban Pastoral Education. He has published four books and numerous articles, has lectured at dozens of seminaries and universities throughout the United States, and has represented the United Church of Christ around the world. One of Chicago's most influential community leaders, he has received three Presidential Commendations.

Rev. Addie L. Wyatt is a founder and co-pastor emeritus of the Vernon Park Church of God. She was "Woman of the Year" of *Time* magazine (1975) and *Ladies Home Journal* (1977), and was one of *Ebony* magazine's "100 Most Influential Black Americans" from 1980 to 1984. Working closely with Dr. Martin Luther King Jr., she participated in civil rights marches in Selma, Chicago, and Washington, D.C. Rev. Wyatt was appointed by Eleanor Roosevelt to the Commission on the Status of Women and became a major force behind the Equal Rights Amendment and Equal Pay for Equal Work. She was international vice president of both the United Food and Commercial Workers Union and the Amalgamated Meat Cutters and Butcher Workmen of North America. She was also a founder of Operation Push, the Coalition of Labor Union Women, and the National Organization for Women.

Don Wycliff is public editor of the *Chicago Tribune*. He previously served for nine years as its editorial page editor, during which time it won a Pulitzer Prize, was a finalist for another, and won two Distinguished Writing Awards from the American Society of Newspaper Editors. Mr. Wycliff came to the *Tribune* from the *New York Times* where he was a member of the editorial board for five years and wrote on a wide range of issues, including social policy, education, religion, and race relations. Earlier he had worked as an editor of the *New York Times' Week in Review* section and as a reporter or editor at several other newspapers, including the *Chicago Daily News* and the *Chicago Sun-Times*. A Texas native educated in Catholic schools in several states, he earned his bachelor's degree at the University of Notre Dame and later attended graduate school at the University of Chicago.

Rev. Seiichi Michael Yasutake was a priest at St. Matthew's Episcopal Church in Evanston, Illinois, and St. Peter's Episcopal Church in Chicago. Born and raised in Seattle, he was (for one-and-a-half years) one of thousands of Japanese Americans imprisoned in U.S. government internment camps during World War II. Having declared himself a conscientious objector opposed to war, he was then expelled from the University of Cincinnati when federal authorities challenged his "loyalty." He later attended Boston University (B.A.), Seabury-Western Theological Seminary (M.Div. and D.Div.), and Loyola University (Ph.D.). He worked for the return of American Indian land, for Puerto Rican independence, and on behalf of countless victims of racism. As executive director of the *Interfaith Prisoners of Conscience Project,* he aided Americans imprisoned for political reasons.

Richard Young is the violist of the Vermeer Quartet. He studied with Josef Gingold, Aaron Rosand, Zoltan Szekely, and William Primrose. At the age of thirteen he was invited to perform for Queen Elisabeth of Belgium. He has since been soloist with various orchestras and has given recitals throughout the United States. A special award winner in the Rockefeller Foundation American Music Competition, he was a violinist with the Rogeri Trio and the New Hungarian Quartet. A fellow of the Royal College of Music in Manchester, England, he has taught at Northern Illinois University, Northwestern University, the University of Michigan, and was chairman of the string faculty at Oberlin Conservatory. Mr. Young has done extensive volunteer work in the inner city for the People's Music School and the International Music Foundation, for whom he supervises an outreach program in the arts-starved Chicago public schools. The producer of the Vermeer Quartet's CD of *The Seven Last Words of Christ,* he has organized all their public performances of this work.

Dr. Grover A. Zinn is associate dean of the College of Arts and Sciences and the William H. Danforth Professor of Religion at Oberlin College. He received his B.A. in physics from Rice University, a B.D. from the Divinity School of Duke University, and a Ph.D. from Duke University.

He is an ordained minister of the United Methodist Church. Dr. Zinn has written on medieval Christian mysticism, iconography, and theology, and is the coeditor of *Medieval France: An Encyclopedia* (Garland, 1995). His translation of the writings of Richard of St.-Victor, a twelfth-century French mystic, appears in *Classics of Western Spirituality*. The recipient of a fellowship from the National Endowment for the Humanities, he has twice received H. H. Powers grants from Oberlin to photograph European cathedrals, monasteries, and pilgrimage sites. He is one of the organizers of a conference, Saint-Denis Revisited, at the Index of Christian Art, Princeton University. He is currently serving for a second term on the council of the Medieval Academy of America, and has been elected twice to the council of the American Society of Church History.

APPENDIX

VERMEER STRING QUARTET

Shmuel Ashkenasi, violin
Mathias Tacke, violin
Richard Young, viola
Marc Johnson, cello

With performances in practically every major city in North America, Europe, Japan, and Australia, the Vermeer Quartet has achieved an international stature as one of the world's finest ensembles. Formed in 1969 at Marlboro, its members are originally from Israel, Germany, New York, and Nebraska, thus providing a unique blend of musical and cultural backgrounds. Switzerland's *Suisse* writes, "Out of this alchemy is born a thing of beauty which one can define, without hesitation, as perfection."

The Vermeer has performed at virtually all the most prestigious festivals, including Tanglewood, Aldeburgh, Norfolk, Aspen, Mostly Mozart, Bath, South Bank, Lucerne, Stresa, Flanders, Kneisel Hall, Caramoor, Santa Fe, Albuquerque, Berlin, Schleswig-Holstein, Orlando, Edinburgh, Great Woods, Spoleto, Ravinia, and the Casals Festival. Based in Chicago, they spend part of each summer on the coast of Maine as the featured ensemble for Bay Chamber Concerts. The Vermeer has been associated with Northern Illinois University as "resident artist faculty" since 1970. They are also Fellows of the Royal

Northern College of Music in Manchester, England, where they have presented annual master classes since 1978.

The Vermeer Quartet has performed well over two hundred works, including nearly all the "standard" string quartets, many lesser-known compositions, a number of contemporary scores, and various other works with guests. Their discography includes the complete quartets of Beethoven, Tchaikovsky, and Bartók, plus additional works by Schubert, Mendelssohn, Dvorak, Verdi, Shostakovich, Haydn, Tchaikovsky, Schnittke, and Brahms. About their Beethoven recordings, *Stereo Review* says, "What these peerless players give us is a heady blend of old-fashioned warmth and communicativeness, with exemplary demonstrations of modern standards of both taste and technique. More persuasive performances of any of these quartets are simply not to be found." The Vermeer's Grammy-nominated recording of *The Seven Last Words of Christ* has been broadcast to over 60 million listeners worldwide, thus demonstrating an enduring appeal that reaches far beyond the traditional classical music audience. The *American Record Guide* calls this CD "an experience unlike any other."

The Vermeer String Quartet's Grammy-nominated CD of Franz Joseph Haydn's *The Seven Last Words of Christ* is available from Alden Productions: CD 23042. On this special two-disk set, CD #1 follows Haydn's original format whereby each section of music is preceded by a spoken introduction. The speakers include Virgil P. Elizondo, Martin E. Marty, Raymond E. Brown, Dallin H. Oaks, T. L. Barrett, Kelly Clem, Martin Luther King Jr., and Jason Robards. CD #2 presents the music only, with all the repeats. A cassette version of CD #1 [CS 23044] is also available. For information on how these recordings may be purchased, consult the Vermeer's website:

www.vermeerqt.com

Two CDs are included with this book. CD #2 consists of brief recorded examples which illustrate the section entitled *The Words and the Music.*

CD #1 is a complete presentation of Haydn's *The Seven Last Words of Christ* featuring speakers who have appeared with the Vermeer Quartet in various "live" performances over the years.[1]

1	*Introduction*	3:17
	Dick Staub (2004)	
2	Maestoso ed Adagio	6:03
3	*"Father, forgive them, for they know not what they do."*	2:55
	Addie L. Wyatt (2002)	
4	Largo	6:50
5	*"Surely, I say to you, today you will be with me in paradise."*	2:26
	Grover A. Zinn (1997)	
6	Grave e cantabile	5:43
7	*"Woman, behold your son!" "Behold your mother!"*	2:37
	John Buchanan (1998)	
8	Grave	6:45
9	*"My God, my God, why have you forsaken me?"*	3:18
	Jeremiah A. Wright, Jr. (1999)	
10	Largo	5:29
11	*"I thirst."*	1:53
	John Shea (1997)	
12	Adagio	6:40
13	*"It is finished!"*	2:02
	Jean Bethke Elshtain (2002)	
14	Lento	5:31
15	*"Father, into your hands I commend my spirit."*	3:30
	Andrew M. Greeley (1998)	
16	Largo	5:29
17	*The Earthquake*	2:06
	Samuel Betances (1998)	
18	Presto e con tutta la forza	2:06

Total time: 74:58

Con - sum - ma - tum est!